The World of Work Through Children's Literature

The World of Work Through Children's Literature

An Integrated Approach

Carol M. Butzow, Ed.D.

John W. Butzow, Ed.D.

Illustrated by Rhett E. Kennedy

2002
TEACHER IDEAS PRESS
Libraries Unlimited
A Division of Greenwood Publishing Group, Inc.
Greenwood Village, Colorado

To all those who cherish the dignity of work.

TEACHER IDEAS PRESS
Libraries Unlimited
A Division of Greenwood Publishing Group, Inc.
7730 East Belleview Avenue, Suite A200
Greenwood Village, CO 80111
1-800-225-5800
www.lu.com

Library of Congress Cataloging-in-Publication Data

Butzow, Carol M., 1942-
     The world of work through children's literature : an integrated approach / Carol M. Butzow, John W. Butzow ; illustrated by Rhett E. Kennedy
         p. cm.
     Includes bibliographical references and index.
     ISBN 1-56308-814-2 (paper)
     1. Career education. 2. Children's literature--Study and teaching (Elementary) 3. Occupations--Study and teaching (Elementary) 4. Professional--Study and teaching (Elementary) I. Butzow, John W., 1939- II. Title.

LC1037.5 .B88 2002
370.11'3--dc21

                                                                2002020625

Contents

PART II
WORK SKILLS

PART III
WORK COMMUNITIES

Figures

Figure

Preface

The purpose of this book is twofold—to provide activities by which children can practice work-related skills and to provide children with an understanding of the world of work. Students must be helped to acquire both understanding and skills as they learn about the many jobs available in the workplace. By carrying out these goals, a bridge is built between school and what people do for work.

Teachers are limited in the number of firsthand working situations they can experience and use as a basis for lessons in the classroom. There also is not ample time to delve into career education topics as a separate entity. To facilitate a connection between the world of work and the school child, we recommend using works of children's literature as a springboard to learning. The use of stories is a familiar and effective vehicle of instruction. Stories make it easy for children to imagine workplace situations that they have not yet personally experienced. Stories also integrate the world of work with subject-specific activities and allow students to build on their own knowledge of the topic.

For example, *Mommy's Office* by Barbara Shook Hazen, is an excellent story that shows a contemporary workplace. The mother is a "knowledge worker" who provides a service, rather than a specific product, to a commercial client. She uses presentations and explanatory skills in providing that service. While we are not told the nature of the business, it is most likely marketing, advertising, or a similar enterprise.

The child in the story who spends the day in the office with Mommy is shown engaging in similar age-appropriate activities such as interacting with people, and drawing her own "presentation." She has practiced skills of observation and expression as they relate to her own reality. These are the same skills the mother uses in the adult world to convince customers of their need for this service. The juxtaposition of the two females answers the questions, "What is to be learned?" and "Why must it be learned?"

Teaching about the world of work in elementary schools is challenging because of time constraints. By using children's literature we can integrate work-related topics into the existing curriculum and provide activities that aid children in becoming familiar with the world of work and understanding why its many aspects will be important to them.

Introduction

During the past decade, our emphasis as authors has been on developing units for teaching science through children's literature. It was with that in mind that we looked at *The Bobbin Girl*—a story that takes place during the Industrial Revolution in Massachusetts. The story and its presentation immediately attracted us, yet it did not fit into our science format. We discussed the book and agreed that it could be developed into an excellent unit but with a different emphasis. It was from this discussion that the "world of work" evolved.

As we began collecting a number of books with work-related themes, we found great diversity in the way this topic was handled. These books did not give the simple job-description treatment of an occupation. Sophisticated themes covered included economics, technology, women in the workplace, barter, the labor movement, and labor unions.

As in our past work, we have chosen fictional works of children's literature with story lines that help youngsters assimilate the concepts covered in the unit. Each book is presented as an integrated unit, touching all areas of the curriculum. The grade levels we have targeted are K–4, but many of the books could also be used in fifth and sixth grade (e.g., *The Bobbin Girl* and *Waiting for the Evening Star*).

We recommend that, unless otherwise indicated, activities be performed by the students rather than simply demonstrated by the teacher. Hands-on, active learning should be encouraged as students develop their own understandings and construct their knowledge of the topic. Each unit is a compilation of activities that is offered to the teacher to be taught along with the school curriculum or objectives. They are not meant to stand alone as units of instruction. The number of activities suggested for each unit would be too numerous for a workable lesson plan.

In each unit you will find a list of concepts and related words. Each chapter begins with a summary of a selected work of children's literature. Next is a list of chapter concepts related to the content of the story. This is followed by a list of unit words found in the text, as well as words related to the text. For example, the word *occupation* is not found in most of the selected books, but examples of occupations are described in many of the books such as in *Worksong*. There are suggestions for teaching language arts, science, math, social studies, art or music, and library and computer skills. Background-building activities and references are also included to help the students construct their understanding of the story's theme.

The 23 chapters of the book are divided into 3 parts based on the particular aspects of the world of work—the local economy, work skills, and work communities. In Part I, for example, *The Milkman's Boy* deals with mechanizing a family-run dairy; *Potato: A Tale of the Great Depression* chronicles how one family copes with hard times.

Part II centers on the skills of the worker. For example, the schoolteacher in *Lilly's Purple Plastic Purse*, the woodworker in *Workshop*, the migrant worker in *Working Cotton*, and the office management team member in *Mommy's Office* all have special skills that they contribute to their jobs. These books also demonstrate that people can take pride in the work they do.

Part III focuses on work communities within the Amish community in *Raising Yoder's Barn* and the division of labor in a village in Cameroon, Africa, in *The Village of Round and Square Houses*. Without the support from the community, these societies would not exist as they do.

The production assembly line, labor unions, job-related relocation, barter economy, the home as workplace, marketing tactics, and the concept of shift work are among the many topics covered in this book. You teach those units that best fit into your curriculum and fill your agenda needs. We hope that this study of the "world of work" will increase student awareness of and interest in the world of work and empower students to develop the work-related skills they will need in the future.

PART I

THE LOCAL ECONOMY

CHAPTER 1

Albert's Field Trip

Leslie Tryon
New York: Atheneum, 1993

Summary

Everything at Georgie and Gracie's apple farm was informative and delicious. Still, the best part of the day was the hug before going to bed.

Theme

The numerous uses of the apple provide many different kinds of people the opportunity to make a living. Extra value is added to the market value of the apple because of additional work done at the farm by the workers.

Content Related Concepts

production line, conveyer belt, division of labor

Content Related Words

codling worm, hose, spout, sapling, categories

Activities

1. Two questions can be answered after reading this book: (a) Who was Albert? and (b) What was the best part of the day? Ask the children if they agree on the answers.

2. Is there an apple orchard or other farm located nearby? If so, organize a field trip there. The yellow pages or the local Chamber of Commerce might be of help in finding one.

3. Get a local map from the Chamber of Commerce, make copies, and have the children find the apple orchard and trace a path for getting there. What are the names of the roads that will be traveled? Students can make a list. If students are too far from a farm, have them visit a market and make observations in the fresh produce section. Plan the route to the grocery store, substituting city street names for the roads in the country.

4. As part of the field trip to an apple orchard or the visit to a grocery store, have the children bring in a permission slip signed by their parent or guardian (Figure 1.1). Some parents may be able to help with the trip (e.g., arranging transportation, accompanying the children, making lunch arrangements, setting up rules of conduct, and directing

follow-up activities). Before the day of the trip, be sure that students have reviewed the different stages of production they will see (e.g., apples being grown, cultivated, picked, sorted by kind and size, packed for shipment, used for juice and baking, and sold to customers).

PERMISSION SLIP

September 8

My child_____has my permission to visit Stoney Acre Orchards on Friday, September 23. I understand that each child should wear a jacket or sweater. Snacks will be provided. Children will arrive back at the Eisenhower School at 4:30 and should be picked up at the front door.

Signature of parent or guardian_____

Figure 1.1. Apple orchard permission slip.

5. Before leaving, ask the music teacher to suggest "school-bus riding songs." These could include ones with fun-to-sing repeating verses, such as "I Know an Old Woman Who Swallowed a Fly." Or perhaps work songs, such as "I've Been Working on the Railroad," that the children know. Do they know any songs about apples?

6. The apple farm is an example of a production line. What does this mean? Have students look up the definition in a dictionary. Why is it better to have a production line than to have each person do every step of the process from start to finish? Have students discuss this or write down the reasons.

7. At the farm in *Albert's Field Trip*, the apples were put into categories according to kind and size. Why? What is a "category"? What other categories could apply to the apples (e.g., color, variety, freshness). A similar task can be performed in the classroom using fruit, nuts, beans, pasta, or other items.

8. What kinds of jobs are available at the apple farm? Who does the work (e.g., day laborers, migrant workers)? What kinds of job skills are needed?

9. Have the children work in groups to make a flow chart based on their experiences at the apple farm. This flow chart should show the production and use of apples from the tree to the home (see Figure 1.2).

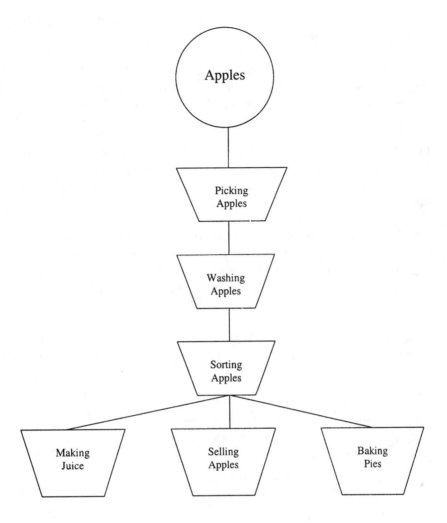

Figure 1.2. Apple products flow chart.

10. Apples are sold in grocery stores or at fruit stands. In what are they packaged? How many pounds of apples are in a bag? What is the price per pound? Why are some apples displayed in loose piles? Is there an advantage to this? What do the loose apples cost per pound? Ask a volunteer to bring in a list of prices of various apples at one or two stores or fruit stands. Rank these from the most expensive to the least expensive per pound.

11. "An apple a day, keeps the doctor away." Are apples really good for your health? Study the nutritional label on a bag of apples and answer these questions: Would an apple be a good snack for a dieter? Will apples raise your cholesterol? How many grams of fat are in an apple? Are apples a good source of dietary fiber? Are they high in sodium? A good source of protein? What conclusions can students draw about the nutritional value of an apple?

12. Have slices of different varieties of apples available for the children to taste (e.g., Delicious, MacIntosh, Jonathan). What kinds of apples are they? Ask children to describe the difference in taste between the apples. Which apples are their favorites?

13. What are apples used for? Make some tasty treats using apples (e.g., apple pie, applesauce, apple crisp, apple salad). Does anyone have another favorite apple treat?

14. Some stores also carry dried apples. Bring in some and have the children taste a few pieces. What do dried apples taste like? Why are apples dried? How are they used? Caution: Teachers should be aware of students' food allergies.

15. If the skin is peeled from an apple and the apple is left to sit, it will turn brown and not be as tasty. Leave a bowl of apple slices to sit out on a table. In another bowl, sprinkle the apples with lemon juice or concentrate and stir them to coat. Leave these apples to sit out also. What observations can be made? Are brown apples less satisfactory? Why?

16. Another activity involves leaving apples in a bowl in the classroom while keeping a similar bowl of apples in the refrigerator. The apples will take several days or even weeks to show a difference. What does this indicate about how to keep apples? Does this explain why, in *Albert's Field Trip*, the temperature in the storage room was so low?

17. Help the children visualize the 35-degree temperature in the storage room by discussing the clothing they would wear at that temperature and what outdoor activities would be appropriate. Do other foods get stored at cool temperatures? What happens to the food if the temperature goes below freezing? What if it is too warm?

18. Have students create personalized stationery by making apple prints on paper. The apple is cut in half horizontally so that the core is exposed. The apple half is thinly brushed with tempera or acrylic paint and then pressed onto the sheet of paper. Holes left by the apple seeds will form a pattern in the middle of the apple. Note: Remember that apples can be green or yellow, as well as red, when selecting colors for the prints.

19. An apple mobile, like the one in Figure 1.3, can be made using the apple pattern in Figure 1.4. Colored construction paper (red, green, or yellow) is used for the outside and white for the inside. Seeds may be drawn or pasted on the core piece. Tie the sections together with yarn or string leaving two or three inches between each piece. Suspend the mobiles from the ceiling.

20. Using the personalized stationery from Activity 18 or a large cutout of an apple (Figure 1.5), have the children write about their day at the apple farm and write thank-you notes to the workers at the orchard.

Figure 1.3. Apple mobile design.

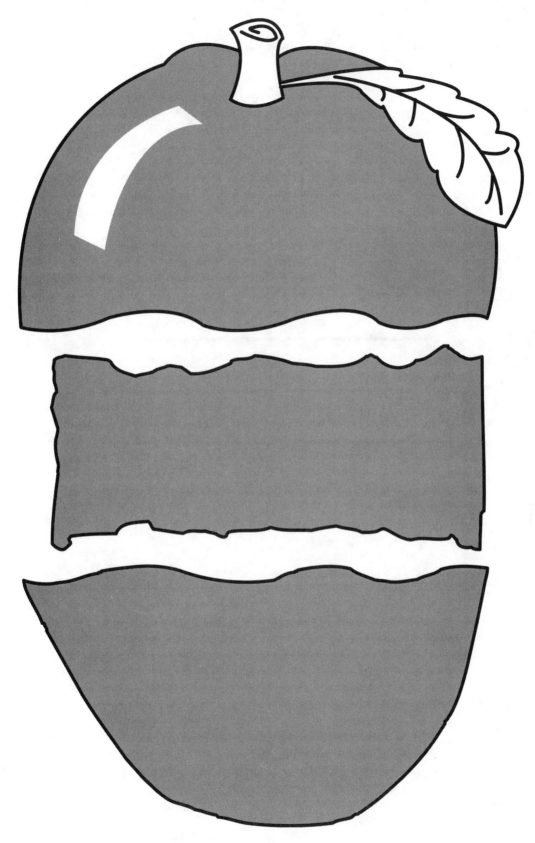

Figure 1.4. Apple mobile pattern.

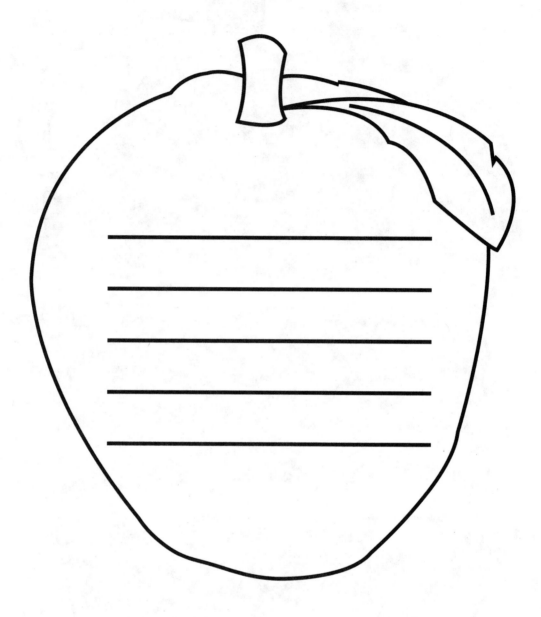

Figure 1.5. Apple writing form.

21. What does it mean to be "the apple of my eye"? Where is "the Big Apple"? Why do people say they "can't compare apples to oranges"? Do parents or teachers know more sayings about apples? What do they mean?

22. Obtain an apple sapling to plant in the school yard or nearby park. The teacher will need to get permission to do a planting. Check with the park service or school administration. Students may choose between a fruit-bearing apple or an ornamental crab apple tree. Do they differ in care requirements? Is one faster growing? Which grows taller? What will happen to the apples that fall to the ground in the autumn? Note: To pay for the apple tree, students could conduct a fund raising project or ask the PTA for funding.

23. Where are apples grown commercially? Have the children find references to apple growing in the Library Media Center or by using the Internet. Web sites from Michigan and Washington apple growers are given here: http://www.bestapples.com or http://michiganapples.com/.

24. Word Search

    These are the words in the word search (Figure 1.6, page 10).

Red Delicious	Granny Smith	Cortland	MacIntosh
Jonathan	Rome	Northern Spy	Gala
Baldwin	Empire	Winesap	Fuji
Ida Red			

    Note: Because the differences among the varieties of apples can be so subtle in nature, there are no clues given to distinguish them. Teachers may wish to introduce a limited number of apples to the children and identify them by specific characteristics of sight and taste.

References

Gibbons, Gail. *The Seasons of Arnold's Apple Tree*. Orlando, FL: Harcourt, Brace, 1984.

Wallace, Nancy. *Apples, Apples, Apples*. Bichester, Oxfordshire: Winslow Press, 2000.

```
N A H T A N O J G K D S N H Y E F Z O W
N Y K I H L E D Q J H S O T N I C A M T
L A M M J X V O Y C Y K S K X J J V W D
F Z U E I U V F K B P V B D Z J B R D U
Y X E R Y H F U B N S V V K V U B P V L
Q K O A U D Q P U L N V A N Q V A S S X
X R G H E T Y W E B R G L Y X S M U O A
A J X R J B T H A X E P A Z E Z R O M Y
P M A X A C W L B D H O G N A E W I M D
F D G S N K D F W S T S I T A Z I C Y R
I P R L V W W Q E C R W F H V X N I K G
Q Y A X I G T A Q O O H U D N D Y L M O
F U N N B N A I S R N X D K E D T E A K
V Q N E E U W K W T W H H J E L Z D A L
J P Y C M O S F W L D N Z M B N A D I V
R F S P Z P A U U A I V O R E T C E Y B
A P M H F J I N O N U R P I E Y V R U D
M A I Q G N D R X D E P P J V W A M I B
Y N T S J L S I E N O M N D E N R E J K
Y Z H G L T B E Q P R P S J J U T A G T
```

Figure 1.6. Apple word search.

CHAPTER 2

Potato:
A Tale of the Great Depression

Kate Lied

Washington, DC: National Geographic Society, 1997

Summary

Dorothy was born during the Great Depression. Her father lost his job and the bank took away their house. To make money, her parents borrowed a car and money for gas. They went to Montana and camped out while they picked potatoes. When the day's work was over, they picked potatoes for themselves and took them back to Iowa to buy things they needed. Eventually, Dorothy's father got a new job and they moved to Washington, DC, where things were better for the family.

Theme

To make a living it is necessary to go where the jobs are. Poor economic conditions may require people to move or work away from their homes.

Content Related Concepts

Great Depression, unemployment, economic recovery

Content Related Words

foreclose, mortgage, burlap sacks, dashboard, running board

Activities

1. On a map, trace Dorothy's journey from Iowa to Montana, back to Iowa, to Washington, DC and then to Hawaii (see Figure 2.1 and page 151 in the Appendix). Have children in the class traveled in another state or lived elsewhere? Locate these states. Which are most frequently mentioned? Help the children graph these.

2. Which states are famous for growing potatoes? Have the children check at home on potato bags to see where they are from. Locate these states. Do they have anything in common? Does the encyclopedia give the name of other states?

Figure 2.1. Map of the United States.

3. In Aroostook County, Maine, students were once hired to pick potatoes during the fall harvest. To do this they were absent from school for 3 or 4 weeks in September or October. The time missed in school was made up by starting the fall semester in early August. Can the class guess how this would affect the lives of the students in Maine? Note: The students were paid to pick the potatoes.

4. There are many varieties of white potatoes (e.g., red-skinned potatoes) as well as sweet potatoes and yams. All of these potatoes are examples of foods containing carbohydrates, which produce energy in humans when eaten. Test various foods to see if they are carbohydrates by putting a drop of iodine on them. If it turns dark blue, it is a carbohydrate. Consult the food pyramid to see how many carbohydrates people should eat in a day. Note: There is a food pyramid shown in Chapter 3, *The Milkman's Boy* (Figure 3.1). Teachers will need to instruct the children to keep the iodine off of their fingers and clothes as the stain is enduring. Children should be cautioned against ingesting any iodine.

5. Have a volunteer visit the grocery store to get prices of different varieties of potatoes as well as sweet potatoes and yams. How much difference in price is there? How does the price of a 5-pound bag compare to a 10-pound bag or a 25-pound bag? Which potatoes are the best bargain? Are sweet potatoes more expensive than white ones? Note: Probably several different brands will be represented, which will make comparison shopping more of a challenge.

6. Cut a potato into several pieces making sure that each piece has an eye. Plant the eye in a cup of soil and care for it as with any plant. A potato vine will grow. Note: A new sweet potato vine will also grow if the tip of the potato (about one to two inches) is submerged in water and placed in a sunny window.

7. The Great Depression began in 1929 and lasted until the mid-1930s. To see how long ago this was, put a knot in a ball of twine every 10 inches; each space between knots represents 10 years. How many knotted spaces will be needed to go back to 1929? Use this method to date other important events. Note: The teacher may wish to use increments of 1 or 5 years to represent each knotted section because students may be under 10 years old (see Figure 2.2).

8. In an economic depression, many people lose their jobs. They do not have money to pay for their houses or to buy food and clothing. During the Great Depression, many people got help from relatives or other people in their town who were more fortunate. How was Dorothy's family affected by the depression? Why did the bank foreclose on their home? How did her father find another job? What kind of job was it? How did her father and mother work to solve these problems?

9. How did the children during the Great Depression think they could help to make money if there were economic problems at home? Was there a way to earn money? Was Dorothy a help to her mom and dad during this time?

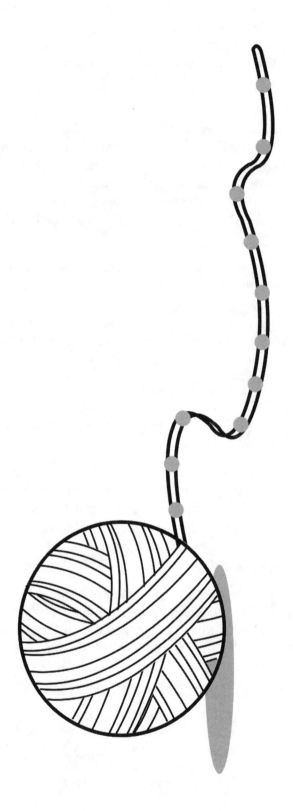

Figure 2.2. Twine time line.

10. There are still some people living today who were alive at the time of the Great Depression. Many have fascinating stories about life at that time. They will never forget how their lives were changed by this event. Invite an older person to talk to the class about life during this period of time. Have the children make up questions ahead of time for the speaker. Note: If transportation to the school is a problem, arrange a telephone interview or tape the answers to the questions that the children have written.

11. Some people who lived through the Great Depression say that they were not as affected by the situation because they lived on a farm. Why would it be better to live on a farm during a depression? Are there advantages to living on a farm today? Were there other jobs that were less affected by the Great Depression? Which jobs were greatly affected? Note: You may want to explain to the children that paper currency lost its value at this time, and many people resorted to trade by barter.

12. This book was written by an 8-year-old girl as part of a writing contest. Have the children organize a writing contest for the school. Many decisions will need to be made (e.g., age categories, topics for writing, dates of entry, judging criteria, selection of judges, prizes).

13. The Great Depression was one of the most tragic events of the 1930s. But there were many good things that occurred during this period of time (e.g., "The Star Spangled Banner" was officially adopted as the national anthem, Amelia Earhardt became the first woman to fly solo across the Atlantic Ocean, Donald Duck was first drawn, Franklin Roosevelt was elected president, women began wearing shorts at the Wimbledon tennis matches, Shirley Temple won a special miniature Oscar for her job in Hollywood movies, superhero comics rose in popularity). Have the children think of some of the entertaining events that have made people smile during their lifetime.

14. One of the few luxuries that people sometimes allowed themselves during the Great Depression was to go to the movies. Child star Shirley Temple was one of the most popular stars of that era. Watch one of her movies, such as *The Little Princess* or *Rebecca of Sunnybrook Farm*. How could these movies be described? Why were her movies so well loved? Are they still popular today?

15. Word Search

    These are the words in the word search (Figure 2.3, page 16).

Tents	Unemployed	Trade	Dashboard
Iowa	Coal mine	Montana	Jobs
Depression	Burlap sack	Eyes	Automobile

References

Harrison, James, and Eleanor Van Zandt. *The Young People's Atlas of the United States.* New York: Kingfisher, 1992.

Jennings, Peter, and Todd Brewster. *The Century for Young People.* New York: Random House (A Doubleday Book for Young Readers), 1999.

```
R O K Y F V X B B E B Z W Z X R P T Z D
T V F R J G A U U R K F P D W C H R W D
U J F A U H B O R L E S G U A C G A L B
E A V A W Q K B L O N M B I H Q F D M X
S T N E T N M I A S I I F T L P K E H R
F Q N H V D M T P V M J F M B F W L Y K
Q A N P Q A E P S H L M U L L U B B J V
H H L A M I V X A R A Q Z P N K B S G S
T A M Q Q L L L C Z O C Y X M L Z A L D
S S W A I F G Z K R C N T Y L I I N A C
J Y D G O S E Y E C N Y H L Z W U A K W
W E M O W S W E A C W D Y P Q W E T H M
C T D X A N H C D A S H B O A R D N L B
C R P A H U U M D G G P J O B S S O K O
G M W N Z Y D E P R E S S I O N K M B Q
Z X I G K J G C Y H X N X B C N U Z K C
T C G N A T X B L T M M G I W Z C A I D
S C C T R I Z W N P H Q A H J K C C A E
E B L M O O G D E Y O L P M E N U I V S
L X M T J U Z X A L A U T O M O B I L E
```

1. Mom and dad slept in these in Montana __ __ __ __ __

2. Dorothy was born here __ __ __ __ __

3. A period of hard times and few jobs __ __ __ __ __ __ __ __ __ __

4. Persons who did not have a job __ __ __ __ __ __ __ __ __ __

5. Dad worked here until it closed __ __ __ __ __ __ __ __

6. These were used for holding potatoes __ __ __ __ __ __ __ __ __ __

7. To exchange objects __ __ __ __ __ __

8. Potatoes grew here __ __ __ __ __ __ __ __

9. New shoots sprout from these __ __ __ __

10. Potatoes were piled here __ __ __ __ __ __ __ __ __

11. Regular activities done for pay __ __ __ __

12. The family borrowed one for the trip __ __ __ __ __ __ __ __ __ __

Figure 2.3. Potato word search.

CHAPTER 3

The Milkman's Boy

Donald Hall
New York: Walker, 1997

Summary

Father believed that the dairy business could continue without the use of modern technology. It was not until his daughter Elzira was stricken with undulant fever that he listened to the advice of his wife and sons about modernizing the farm. The first step was the pasteurization of milk for their customers.

Theme

Changes in technology can protect health, improve productivity, and increase sales.

Content Related Concepts

family business, consolidation, industrial change, modernization

Content Related Words

dairy, refrigeration, raw milk, pasteurization, perishable foods, icehouse, sawdust, suburbs, Model T, undulant fever

Activities

1. Home delivery of milk was a common practice in the first part of the twentieth century. Increasingly, people have changed to buying their milk at grocery or convenience stores. What happened to cause this change? Where do families of the children in class get their milk? Will it ever become reasonable for people to have home delivered milk again? What changes would have to occur?

2. Milk used to be delivered to homes in glass bottles. Now it comes in paper cartons or plastic jugs. When did this change occur? Why? What are the advantages of paper and plastic instead of glass bottles? Note: Some milk is being bottled in glass bottles again. Why is this so? (Answer: Glass bottles can be heated and sterilized for reuse.)

3. Everyone in the story played a part in the family business. What jobs did each family member do? Was there much leisure time for these people? What were the problems that could occur running a dairy (e.g., the blizzard)?

4. What are the advantages and disadvantages of a family run business as compared to a large, consolidated business run by hired employees? How can computerization of the family business be seen as an asset to the company? Note: Many newspapers print a yearly guide to small family businesses in the area. See if there is one at your local newspaper office. What kinds of businesses are represented? Must they compete with large, consolidated businesses?

5. Ask the Chamber of Commerce for other names of small, independent businesses (e.g., Frank's Shoe Repair, The Flower Gallery, China King Buffet). Note: Large, consolidated businesses might include Kmart, Wendy's, J.C. Penney.

6. Invite one of these people to talk about running a small family business. How is it different from working for someone else? Ask the speaker to comment on Henry's statement: "Start hiring people you don't know and you ask for trouble." Contrast this talk to one by a person from a large nonfamily business. Are they in direct competition?

7. In the story, the father did not want to expand his business or pasteurize the milk. What reasons did he have for not changing? What arguments did his son David have in favor of modernization? Make a chart to compare the ideas of the two men. What are the advantages and disadvantages of the two different sides? Why is the idea of change itself frightening to some people? Have the children cite changes that they are apprehensive about (e.g., going to the next grade, trying out for a sport, visiting relatives).

8. Pasteurization is a process of heating the milk to kill any germs that might be in it. The process was invented by Louis Pasteur and named for him. Read about this man on the Internet or in the Library Media Center. The keywords "Louis Pasteur" will give several accounts of his life.

9. Undulant fever is one of the diseases that can be found in milk. The keywords "undulant fever" will bring you information on the Internet. What were the symptoms of this sickness? What is the treatment for it? Do people still suffer from this disease? Why or why not?

10. Where are the dairies in your area? Locate them on a regional map. Are these large or small dairies? How far does the milk have to travel to the store? Under what conditions does it come so that it does not spoil? What are the advantages and disadvantages of the small and the large dairy? What are the skills necessary to work on a dairy farm? What additional qualifications are necessary to run a dairy farm? Note: Consult local dairy farmers for answers to these questions or contact the local cooperative service.

11. Visit a dairy farm, if possible, or go to a plant that bottles milk. Before the trip, have the children write questions that they would like to have answered. After the trip, write language experience stories as well as a thank you letter to the host or hostess. Note: Children will need to get written permission to go on this field trip.

12. How are the cows milked? How has this changed over the years? Why must the milk be kept cool until it is sent to be pasteurized and bottled?

13. In some states, milk prices are regulated and every dairy must charge the same price. In other areas, the price can vary. Bring in some grocery store flyers. What is the cost of a quart of milk in the local area? Does this vary from store to store? If so, why is there this variation? Note: There are many types of milk and cream (e.g., whole milk, 2% milk, 1% milk, skim milk, whipping cream, half-and-half). Compare the prices of each product in the different stores.

14. Design a milk carton of your own. Create and include your company's name, address, phone number, the size of the carton, nutritional facts, price code, date and any appropriate advertising gimmicks. Note: Use a piece of paper to cover the front of a half-gallon carton or jug. This should give students ample room to include all the information.

15. Have students estimate how much milk a family of four would drink in a week. Measure the amount in gallons and quarts. Note: Remember that a half-gallon is equal to two quarts and a gallon equals four quarts.

16. Have parents help the children answer questions about milk consumption. Which is the most commonly used kind of milk? Do some families drink more than one kind of milk? What is the average price for a quart or gallon of milk in your area? How much money is spent per week for milk? Have the teacher compile the results and help children graph the results. Add other classrooms to the survey to increase the size of the sample. Note: Remember that there are four quarts in a gallon. Use these 5 categories for the survey: Whole milk, 2% milk, 1% milk, skim milk, nonfat dry powdered milk.

17. Does the school serve different kinds of milk? Survey the class to see which kinds they buy. Graph the results. This survey could be expanded to include other classes.

18. Read the information on the panel of the milk carton. The food groups represented are fats, proteins, and carbohydrates. Nutrients include potassium, calcium, vitamin A, and vitamin D. Also shown are the number of calories and the cholesterol content in a serving of milk. Note: The food pyramid uses numbers of servings as an indicator and will include dairy products such as cheese. See Figure 3.1.

19. The author of *The Milkman's Boy*, Donald Hall, is an accomplished poet who lives in New Hampshire. Have the children write a poem about topics in the book (e.g., the three horses, Paul's delivery route, the great blizzard).

Figure 3.1. Food pyramid.

20. Locate the states, countries, and bodies of water that border New Hampshire. Find some basic facts about this state from the Internet (e.g., population, size). Note: There is also an outline map of the United States in Chapter 2, *Potato: A Tale of the Great Depression*.

21. Ask parents or grandparents if they remember when milk was delivered to the door. Have them share a story with you to bring to class, for example, what happened when the milk was left outside too long? In *The Milkman's Boy*, who always got a ride in the back of Duffy's truck when he came to collect on Saturday morning?

22. Read other books by Don Hall (e.g., *Old Home Day* and *Ox-Cart Man*).

Figure 3.2. Map of New Hampshire.

23. Word Search

    These are the words in the word search (Figure 3.3, page 22).

Dairy	Stable	Milk can	Customers
Horses	Ice house	Undulant fever	Willow bark
Milk	Bottles	Pasteurization	Blizzard
Wagon			

References

Gibbons, Gail. *The Milk Makers*. New York: Atheneum, 1985.

Hall, Donald. *Old Home Day*. San Diego: Browndeer Press, Harcourt Brace, 1966.

———. *Ox-Cart Man*. New York: Viking, 1979.

Halley, Ned. *Farm*. London: Dorling Kindersley, 2000. (An Eyewitness Book)

Harrison, James, and Eleanor Van Zandt. *The Young People's Atlas of the United States*. New York: Kingfisher, 1992.

```
J P E Q X U L W M Y I A U K U U D L S Y
W C I U M V P A S T E U R I Z A T I O N
G M B N F A U A H B L D A D D B O M E D
F U G D P J A K M M O A K N E O K F V C
Y K R U H R A N R K W Q N L Y T F T P
D L T L S J A W M E G X W S N N T R H H
D P H A P T K M V M R G S Y G S Q K I Q
L K O N J B O N W C D E T Z P T U E U W
X P R T K L Q G M I X M A T Q L L V R I
A Y S F E I M U I N M I B L Z E L G C L
P R E E P Z U U L B N L L X R K W N M L
H N S V A Z B E K O I K E R W A G O N O
T O L E P A T N C T I K E F M X Q D M W
Z W F R R R B P A T X O S W O N A O U B
T B V S O D Q T N L V W K D F W J B E A
S Y S P O R I J L E Y R K C E G P O E R
X I L B Q Z L U Q S Y O N S B O K W W K
C U S T O M E R S B M F A E R Y K C L V
I S S N X J T M B T D A I R Y N A K T T
W Y Z K U I C E H O U S E N J N O O J M
```

1. A farm where milk cows are raised
   __ __ __ __ __

2. An important source of calcium __ __ __ __

3. Milk was delivered in this __ __ __ __ __

4. A building used for keeping horses __ __ __ __ __ __

5. A building used to store ice __ __ __ __ __ __ __ __

6. Glass containers which held milk __ __ __ __ __ __ __

7. They pulled the milk wagon __ __ __ __ __ __

8. Milk was delivered in these containers __ __ __ __ __ __ __

9. A sickness contracted from infected cows or their milk

   __ __ __ __ __ __ __ __ __ __ __ __

10. A process for killing germs in raw milk

    __ __ __ __ __ __ __ __ __ __ __ __ __

11. People who buy goods or services __ __ __ __ __ __ __ __ __

12. A very bad snow storm __ __ __ __ __ __ __ __

13. Natural source of aspirin __ __ __ __ __ __ __ __ __ __

Figure 3.3. Milkman word search.

CHAPTER 4

Mama Is a Miner

George Ella Lyon
New York: Orchard, 1994.

Summary

After the morning rush of getting ready, the children settle onto their school bus, knowing that Mama will soon be deep in the earth with her crew in a coal mine. The children worry for her safety, but she assures them that all will be fine and that it's better than "ringin' up grub."

Theme

Mama takes a job in the coal mines because her job at the supermarket isn't enough to pay the bills.

Content Related Concepts

coal mining, women in the workplace, nontraditional jobs

Content Related Words

miner, mantrip, battery pad, cable

Activities

1. Several weeks before starting the unit, place a lump of coal into a clear plastic or glass bottle and cover it with water. Let the coal stand. In time, the water will become discolored and polluted as minerals are leached out of the coal. This shows what happens when water runs through coal mines. The water eventually reaches streams and rivers and changes them to a bright coppery orange color. The expense of cleaning up this pollution is enormously expensive. Who is responsible for this pollution? Who should clean it up? Should we even bother?

Figure 4.1. Pollution bottle.

2. Ask the American Coal Foundation to send materials for teaching about coal. Teachers may access this website: http://www.acf-coal.org/.

3. Coal deposits are in many states in America. One group of sites includes Pennsylvania, West Virginia, Kentucky, Tennessee, Ohio, and Alabama. A second group includes Illinois, Indiana, and a part of Kentucky. The third group is comprised of Missouri, Iowa, Kansas, and Oklahoma. There are also smaller coal deposits in North Dakota, South Dakota, Montana, Wyoming, Utah, Colorado, Arizona, and New Mexico. On a map of the United States locate these states. Note: There is an outline map of the United States in the Chapter 2, *Potato: A Tale of the Great Depression.*

4. Are the states grouped together or are they scattered? Are these areas mountainous or flat? Note: Remember that coal mining can be done underground or on the surface of the earth in "strip mines." What is the difference between underground mining and strip mining?

5. There are large deposits of coal in Europe. Coal is found in England, Scotland, Wales, France, Belgium, Germany, Poland, the Czech Republic, Hungary, and the countries of the former Soviet Union. Locate these countries on a large classroom wall map. Explain why there are many ethnic groups found in coal producing areas of the United States, for example, there is a concentration of Welsh coal miners in Pennsylvania.

6. The United States was once a leading producer of coal for the world. How was coal used in the past? What prevents coal from being used that way now? How is coal used today? Reference books in the Library Media Center can help.

7. In recent years, coal production has dwindled. Why? When the mines close, what happens to the miners and their families? What assistance can be given to these people?

8. The coal industry is being attacked as the source of acid rain, global warming, and the greenhouse effect. In the Library Media Center, find a working definition of these three conditions. How do they contribute to the pollution problem in the United States?

9. It is only in recent years that women have become coal miners. Many people think that mining is a "man's job" and that there is no place for women in the mines. Other "men's jobs" included truck driving, construction work, mechanics, law enforcement, middle and upper level management, ministry, president of the United States, and so on. "Women's jobs" were teaching, nursing, secretarial work, homemaking, customer service, hairdressing, etc. Debate this issue. What are the advantages of women going into the mines? What are the disadvantages? Take a vote to see which side wins. Do people vote with their heads or with their hearts? Note: Children may wish to ask parents to cast their vote as well. Tally and graph the results.

10. In the story, Mama used to work "ringing up grub." What does this mean? How would that job be different from working in the mines? What do coal miners do in the mines? How is the seam of coal extracted from the wall of the mine?

11. Why do the miners work in a crew? What are some of the jobs Mama and her crew perform underground? Are there classroom jobs that are best carried out by a crew of

students? Note: It is important to emphasize that coal mining is now very mechanized, and physical strength is not necessarily a requirement to be an effective worker.

12. Throughout history, there were times when miners went "on strike." They refused to work until they got more money and/or better working conditions. Ask the library media specialist to help find information on labor strikes. Have there been any strikes in the local area by coal miners or other groups? What were some of the results of the strike—for the businesses, for the workers, for the public?

13. Coal miners wear a certain type of clothing. These work clothes can be bought at local department stores, working men's stores, discount stores, or through catalogs. Find out the price of a shirt, trousers, and work boots. What is unique about work boots?

14. Use the following price list to simulate selecting clothes. On the list, similar items may be listed at differing costs. This is because more expensive items may indicate better quality. Make a shopping list that does not exceed $250. Select as many items as possible without going over the limit. Note: Clothing items include shirts, pants, thermal underwear, socks, and a belt.

15. Miners work underground where it is always dark except for the light from their lamps. In the winter when the days are short, the miners may not see any hours of sunlight on their way to work or to home. Their days are spent in darkness. How would you feel if you knew you would not see daylight all day long? Does Mama ever say anything about this? How are the students affected when there are fewer hours of daylight during the winter months?

16. Coal mining can present many health hazards, especially to a person's respiratory and skeletal system. Look up "black lung" and "emphysema." How do these diseases affect workers? Can they be cured? How do they affect the worker's quality of life? Why were health benefits one of the major items that coal miners demanded?

17. In coal mining areas, ask a retired coal miner to speak to the class. Write questions to ask before the visit. Note: Unfortunately, in these areas there may be many unemployed miners who would be willing to share their experiences with the class.

18. There is a saying that "Every mother is a working mother." What responsibilities does Mama have besides her job? Why did she quit her job "ringin' up grub"? How does the father help? How do the children help? Have the class make a list of each person's jobs at their home on each day and post them.

19. If all the grownups in the house were working a full time job, how could children help out after school? Could they fix supper? What can they cook? Discuss the responsibilities that different members of the family have. Is the work evenly distributed? How could this be remedied?

20. "Safety first" is a motto used in the mines. What are the dangers associated with going into the mines? How does Mama feel about them? How do her children feel? "Safety first" is also an important motto to remember around the school. Make posters reminding others of safety in the school (e.g., don't run in the hall, don't shove on the playground). Post these in the hallway to share the messages with other classes.

Sale on Work Clothes

WORKPANTS

Regular fit	$24
Or 2 for	$40
Relaxed fit	$30
Denim stretch	$44
Bib overalls	$49

SHIRTS

Cotton/polyester	$20
Or 2 for	$35
100% cotton	$25

THERMAL UNDERWEAR

Tops	$15
Bottoms	$15
2 piece set	$25

THERMAL SOCKS

Single Pair	$6
3 pack	$14

BELT

Standard quality	$14
Extra sturdy	$20

STEEL-TOED BOOTS

Budget quality	$65
Standard quality	$95
Deluxe quality	$155

Figure 4.2. Sale on work clothes.

21. Read other books by George Ella Lyon such as *Cecil's Story*. Compare the role of the mother and the boy with the characters in *Mama Is a Miner*.

22. What Am I?

   The following items appear in *Mama Is a Miner*. Match each word to its definition.

   a. Shift   e. Mantrip   i. One who shovels
   b. "Safety first" f. Continuous miner j. Dinner bucket
   c. Cap light   g. Working face
   d. Tunnel   h. Seam

   _____ 1. a passageway between the main entrance and the work area

   _____ 2. it digs into the earth to bring out minerals

   _____ 3. it takes miners deep into the earth

   _____ 4. it holds a miner's lunch

   _____ 5. the only illumination in the mine

   _____ 6. the surface of the rock to be dug into

   _____ 7. a crevice bearing coal, apart from the surrounding earth

   _____ 8. a block of eight hours comprising the work day

   _____ 9. a slogan heard in coal areas

   _____ 10. one who picks up broken coal and loads it

References

Bartoletti, Susan Campbell. *A Coal Miner's Bride: The Diary of Anetka Kaminska.* New York: Scholastic, 2000.

John, Angela. *Coal Mining Women: Victorian Lives and Campaigns.* Cambridge: Cambridge University Press, 1984.

Lyon, George Ella. *Cecil's Story.* New York: Orchard, 1991.

CHAPTER 5

Gold Fever

Verla Kay

New York: G. P. Putnam's Sons, 1999

Summary

It seemed that everyone was going to prospect for gold in California. When Jasper left his farm to join them, he dreamed of amazing riches. But life did not turn out the way he thought it would, and Jasper became disillusioned with the whole adventure. Gold mining was back-breaking work and Jasper had little to show for his efforts. He was glad to return to his family and farm.

Theme

The cost of living is an important factor in deciding whether workers can afford to work away from home.

Content Related Concepts

forty-niners, gold mining, panning for gold, the Gold Rush

Content Related Words

miner, bedroll, prairie, sagebrush, vultures, canteen, grizzly bear, outcrop, lair, sluice, nugget, brawl, bedrock, boulder, quartz, britches, pocket, vein, profit, inflation

Activities

1. Have the children tell what they think of when they hear the word California, for example, movie stars and beaches. As the teacher reads the book, have them keep in mind their concept of California and compare it to the California in the story. Are there similarities? What are the differences? What would California have looked like in 1849?

2. What was the Gold Rush? Why were these men called the forty-niners? Why were the men in such a hurry to get to California? Who are the modern day forty-niners?

3. It took many months to walk across America to California, which was not yet a state in 1849. On a map, locate the present-day state, along with Sacramento, the city where the gold was discovered at Sutter's Mill. What role does Sacramento play in modern-day California? Note: There is an outline map of the United States in Chapter 2, *Potato: A Tale of the Great Depression*.

4. In the 1800s the journey west was difficult and many of the would-be miners went back home without reaching California. Some died along the way. Make a list of the problems that the travelers faced. Then make a list of problems you might encounter in going across the country today. Compare the two situations.

5. In 1849, 80,000 people emigrated to California. Many of them traveled in large Conestoga wagons that were made in Pennsylvania. These wagons were also called "prairie schooners" because they were similar to large ships that sailed the ocean. Have the children imagine a day's journey in one of these wagons and write about it. Express the sights, sounds, and smells they would encounter. Note: The group might brainstorm this topic together before writing and use the lists made in Activity 4.

6. When gold was found, "inflation" occurred. This meant that the price of goods and services increased. Have half of the children pretend to be prospectors looking for gold. They are coming to town to buy goods. The other half of the class will represent the grocers, restaurant owners, blacksmiths, and so forth, who provide services needed by the men. These shopkeepers must charge money to make a living. The men are looking to make a "profit." With the teacher as moderator, have the two groups debate the question—Why do the prices go up every time someone finds gold? Note: There are clues in the book to help—for example, why do the men in the book appear to be sleeping in tents and not at the hotel?

7. Find information about gold mining in the Library Media Center. Use this along with the book's illustrations to identify tools that the forty-niners used (e.g., pry bar, hammer, nails, buckets, shovels, pick axes, sluice). How do these tools work? Can students identify the six simple machines being used—wedge, lever, screw, pulley, wheel and axle, inclined plane? Note: A lesson on simple machines can be taught using home implements such as a can opener, corkscrew, screwdriver, claw hammer, Venetian blind pull, etc. In most cases the implement will consist of several different simple machines.

8. Gold is a very heavy metal. It weighs 65 pounds per quart. When the miners found gold, it was mixed together with sand, gravel, and dirt. How could the gold pieces be separated from the other materials? Have the children work in small groups to reach a solution and then present their answers. Note: How does gold mining compare to coal mining? For example, where it is done and how the mineral is found.

9. There have been major gold strikes in many different countries (e.g., California 1849, Australia 1851, British Columbia, Canada 1856, South Africa 1886, Alaska 1896). Why were these strikes cause for celebration throughout the world? Look for resources in the Library Media Center for more information on these gold strikes. Locate these places on a large classroom map of the world. Do these places still produce gold commercially?

10. Where is gold mined today? *The World Almanac* gives statistics for each of 11 countries (Figure 5.1). The first figure is the amount of gold produced in that country in 1986; the second figure is the amount produced in 1996. Which country is the largest producer of gold in each of those years? Which of the countries is the smallest gold producer? Between 1986 and 1996 most countries increased their gold production. Which countries did not? Rank the countries by the amount of gold produced in 1986 and 1996. Is there one area of the world where gold is most often found? Students may make additional problems to challenge classmates. Note: Gold production is quoted in troy ounces. The numbers in the chart have been converted to pounds to make it easier for the children to conceptualize the amount of gold. One troy ounce equals 31 grams and there are 454 grams in one pound.

Gold Production
(In Pounds)

Country	1986	1996
Australia	2,500,000	9,300,000
Canada	3,300,000	5,300,000
China	2,000,000	4,700,000
Colombia	1,200,000	700,000
Ghana	300,000	1,600,000
Mexico	250,000	700,000
Philippines	1,300,000	640,000
Russia	8,850,000	3,850,000
South Africa	20,500,000	16,000,000
United States	3,500,000	10,200,000
Zaire	250,000	325,000

Figure 5.1. Gold production table.

11. Why is gold valuable? What are the uses for gold? According to *The World Almanac*, 70 percent of gold is used for jewelry and the arts, 23 percent is used for electronics and other industries, and 7 percent is used in dentistry. Also, the U.S. government holds millions of dollars in gold to back up the value of its money. Make a pie graph to represent these numbers. What does this show us about how gold is used?

12. Most gold is used for artistic purposes, such as jewelry. Have each student design a piece of "gold" jewelry, a statue, a small implement, and the like, which can be made out of clay, flour-and-salt dough, or another malleable substance. Allow the item to dry and then spray with light layers of gold spray paint. Dry.

13. Look for art books in the Library Media Center that show jewelry and other gold articles, for example, the treasures of King Tut in Egypt. Why do the students think these items are so valuable?

14. To wrap up the unit, have a "Gold Fever" dress up day. Students can wear shirts, jeans, vests, boots, and neckerchiefs to copy the look of the forty-niners. Note: Teachers may wish to bring in a few extra neckerchiefs or vests for children who do not have them.

15. Word Search

   These are the words in the word search (Figure 5.2).

Forty-niners	Stream	Mountain	Nugget
Gold	Prairie	Pan	Pry bar
Desert	Sluice	Vein	Tents

References

Harrison, James, and Eleanor Van Zandt. *The Young People's Atlas of the United States.* New York: Kingfisher, 1992.

Schanzer, Rosalyn. *Gold Fever! Tales from the California Gold Rush.* Washington, DC: National Geographic Society, 1999.

```
W R F E J T S J M O U N T A I N P R F Q
E I Q J X L W C A D L O G I C T Y E Y M
S U Y T N H Q M O R O E X K D H Y A C B
U H D D O A Y Z R E C N M T U M C Q V P
E G B X B L P R A I R I E J N U D N M R
Q W Q W N T S E Z Q V Z Z F J K M K V A
N P E B K F O R T Y N I N E R T E P W M
R L W E G S M A X E U R M D Y T Y M U E
E N L U P R A Q L T G N A R E A T C F L
F B I A A C D L Z F G F Z S L U I C E G
M J E E U K C O Q K E C V W Z Y R O S R
G X T E V T Q O V N T L M O B H I F N K
K Q T T L T E S U L I N Z G M O X N M H
F R H J D X B N I J B Z V R B J Y G W R
V T H S K L S F T C D K U J U B D Y D R
Y M B I P F Y U I S E E R A B Y R P H X
K Q F O Q N R B R W D D S T U A H D Q R
X S T R E A M W M H A B X F T T L K M M
R J B D H I O W D H J B E A N F B O K E
K G J F B D E S E R T R N R M M C J J O
```

1. The miners' nickname
   _ _ _ _ _ _ _ _ _ _

2. A valuable mineral _ _ _ _

3. Dry waterless land _ _ _ _ _ _

4. A branch of a river _ _ _ _ _ _ _

5. A large stretch of flat
   land _ _ _ _ _ _ _

6. A man-made channel for
   water _ _ _ _ _ _

7. High elevation of
   land _ _ _ _ _ _ _ _

8. A metal device to separate gold
   nuggets _ _ _

9. A regularly shaped deposit of
   ore _ _ _ _ _

10. A small lump of a
    mineral _ _ _ _ _ _ _

11. A lever for moving
    rocks _ _ _ _ _ _ _

12. The miners slept there _ _ _ _ _ _

Figure 5.2. Gold word search.

CHAPTER 6

Waiting for the Evening Star

Rosemary Wells

New York: Dial Books for Young Readers, 1993

Summary

Bertie felt that everything the family needed was right there on their farm. Anything they didn't have, they could get in trade from the neighbors. He knew when each job was to be done in any season. To him, time went by like a slow song. But his older brother Luke did not share Bertie's feelings and dreamed of a time he could travel beyond the mountains to another world. When Luke boarded the southbound train in 1917, he did not know what lay before him. In his sadness, Bertie felt that he was seeing time itself leave on that train and that life would never be the same.

Theme

Promises of an easier urban life lure people away from the self-sufficiency of rural life.

Content Related Concepts

self-sufficient, barter economy, "store bought"

Content Related Words

haying, milking, paraffin, buttery, sugaring, creamery, huckleberries, pitchfork

Activities

1. More information on Vermont can be found on the Internet using the keywords "Vermont Tourism," or accessing these Web sites: http://www.skivermont.com/ and http://www.vtcheese.com/.

2. In the book, the author acknowledges the help of the Billings Farm and Museum in Woodstock, Vermont, and the Shelburne Museum in Shelburne, Vermont. Using the Internet, find their Web sites. In what parts of the book do the students think the information from these museums would have helped the author?

3. Three communities are mentioned in the book—Barstow, Brattleboro, and Boston. Locate these communities on maps of Vermont (Figure 6.1) and Massachusetts (Figure 22.1, page 138). Do other states, countries, and bodies of water border Vermont?

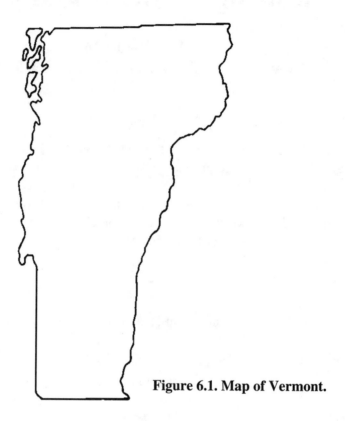

Figure 6.1. Map of Vermont.

4. Bertie says that the year turned like a wheel and that time went by like a slow song. During what events does time seem to go slowly? When does it rush by? Have the children visualize and draw these two scenarios.

5. Numerous jobs were carried out on the farm (e.g., ice cutting, maple sugaring, making mayonnaise, churning butter, growing and harvesting vegetables). Are these jobs still carried out on farms? What are the tasks done on farms today? Where do people get farm products (e.g., ice, maple syrup, mayonnaise, butter and cheese, vegetables) today? A good farmer would need to enjoy doing various tasks on the farm. What other personal qualities would someone need to be a good farmer?

6. In the story, which farm jobs were done indoors? Which ones were done outdoors? Why did the father, the mother, the grandmother, and the children all have to help run the farm? Have the students make a chart showing the members of their own families and the jobs they do around the house. Discuss whether it would be harder to operate a farm or to run a modern home. What reasons do the children have for their decisions?

7. Farm families often used cold frames in which they planted seeds that would grow into seedlings for the garden. To simulate this process in the classroom, plant seeds in disposable aluminum trays and cover them with pieces of glass or clear plastic wrap. Set them out on the sunny side of the building well in advance of the planting season. See the picture of the cold frame in the book for details. Note: Keep the seeds moist and in the sun. The "cold frames" will act like mini-greenhouses to promote early germination and growth of seeds.

8. Farmers hope for good weather so that their crops are not ruined. In the past, many of them depended on the *Old Farmers' Almanac* for weather forecasts. To find out more about this book, write to Box 520, Dublin, NH 03444, call 603-563-8111, or access the Web site: http://almanac.com/. Many articles there about farming and other topics may be of interest to the reader. Do farmers still use the Almanac? Why or why not?

9. Bertie didn't think that the winter food was very good, for example, the beans and suet pudding. The major reason why people ate these foods was that there was no way to preserve food using refrigeration. Bring in some flyers from the local appliance store and comparison shop for refrigerators or freezers. What are some of the features of the various refrigerators (e.g., size, capacity, price)? What foods would the children have to give up if there were no refrigerators or freezers (e.g., ice cream, fresh salads, milk)? How did the people preserve food before refrigeration (e.g., canning, drying, pickling, salting)?

10. Why does Luke want to leave the farm? Does he have any future plans in mind? Ask the children if they would like to move away from their town after they are grown up. Separate the class into those who would like to stay and those who would like to leave. Have each group prepare a list of reasons for their decision and share these in a discussion or debate.

11. If people are satisfied with their jobs, they will probably not move away. But if employment opportunities are better somewhere else, they may leave. Ask someone from the Chamber of Commerce or tourist bureau to speak on the job situation in your town. Are there jobs for everyone who wants to work? What types of jobs are available? Are these jobs that require special skills or training? Are these highly paid jobs? Is there a chance for advancement? What jobs can the students expect to find there in the future?

12. Bertie does not want Luke to leave so he tries to convince him that they have everything they need on the farm in Vermont. What things did Bertie say they had? Would today's students be satisfied with these? What might today's students feel is essential to life? Have the children differentiate between things they "need" and things they "want."

13. The book ends as Luke boards the train to go to war. We do not know what happens to him. Does he return to the farm? Is he killed in the war? Does he settle in Boston? Have the children pretend to be Bertie, the younger brother, and write a sequel to this book, explaining what happened to Luke.

14. Today, Vermont is famous for two of its farm products—cheese and maple syrup. Imagine that the school's Parent-Teacher Association has allotted $350 to buy "thank you" gifts for each of the school's 10 parent volunteers. Each child is to compile a $35 gift basket of cheeses, syrups, or other items. The gift will be mailed to the volunteer's home. Contents may include:

3 lbs. Cheese $20	24 pcs. Maple candy $12
1 lb. Cheese $8	8 oz. Fruit jam $5
½ lb. Cheese $5	6 oz. Maple mustard $5
32 oz. Maple syrup $40	7 oz. Biscuit crackers $6 or 2 for $10
16 oz. Maple syrup $28	

Note: Cheese comes in many varieties, including: Sharp cheddar, mild cheddar, smoked, and jack cheese. Jam is raspberry, cranberry, or blueberry. Encourage students to select a variety of gifts and to use all of the money allotted. All prices include shipping.

15. Grandma Moses (1860–1961) was a farmer's wife who began painting after she was in her seventies. Her pictures show scenes that are very similar to the countryside in Vermont. Her style of painting is called "primitivism." The Bennington Museum, in Bennington, Vermont, has the largest public collection of Grandma Moses works. To see some of these, access the museum at http://www.benningtonmuseum.com/. For more information on Grandma Moses and primitivism, look in an encyclopedia, in art books in the Library Media Center, or on the Internet. Have the children experiment with this manner of painting.

16. In an acrostic, the letters of the word are written top to bottom. Each letter begins a word, which describes the topic. Here is one using the word "Vermont" for a topic. Use other topics in the unit to make acrostics.

Very cold in winter

Early vegetables in a cold frame

Raising animals for the fair

Maple syrup on snow

Overlooking Lake Champlain

Night skies are filled with stars

Time goes by like a slow song

Green Mountain Shop
Box 752
Brattleboro, VT

Customer's Name: _____

Address: _____

City, State, Zip: _____

Daytime phone: _____

Ship To (if different from above): _____

Address: _____

City, State, Zip: _____

Item	Quantity	Color/Size/Weight	Unit Price	Total Price

For all orders: Method of Payment

Merchandise total   Personal Check _____

_____   Money Order _____

Shipping and   Credit Card _____
handling_____
                                                       Visa_____ Master Card _____
Sales Tax 6% for VT
customers_____   Discover _____ AmEx _____

Total   Account Number
Sale_____
                                                  _____

                                                  Expiration Date

                                                  _____

                                                  Signature of Card

                                                  Holder_____

Figure 6.2. Products order form.

17. Math Puzzle
Find the letter that is equal to each number. Use these numbers to fill in the blanks. This will be Grandmother's advice to Bertie.

A	B	C	D	E	F	G	H	I	J	K	L	M
1	2	3	4	5	6	7	8	9	10	11	12	13

N	O	P	Q	R	S	T	U	V	W	X	Y	Z
14	15	16	17	18	19	20	21	22	23	24	25	26

25 15 21   23 1 9 20   6 15 18   20 8 1 20

___ ___ ___   ___ ___ ___ ___   ___ ___ ___   ___ ___ ___ ___

5 22 5 14 9 14 7   19 20 1 18   14 15 23

___ ___ ___ ___ ___ ___ ___   ___ ___ ___ ___   ___ ___ ___

References

Halley, Ned. *Farm.* London: Dorling Kindersley, 2000. (An Eyewitness Book)

Harrison, James, and Eleanor Van Zandt. *The Young People's Atlas of the United States.* New York: Kingfisher, 1992.

PART II

WORK SKILLS

CHAPTER 7

The Paperboy

Dav Pilkey

New York: Orchard, 1996

Summary

A boy gets up early in the morning to deliver newspapers. When he is finished, he goes back to bed as the rest of the world wakes up.

Theme

Children can be part of the work force. The newspaper boy demonstrates a number of important skills and abilities required by his job.

Content Related Concepts

Responsibility, companionship

Content Related Words

Morning Star Gazette, news carrier, paper route, newspaper bag

Activities

1. Many newspapers have the name *Gazette*. Others are called the Tribune, Times, Herald, Dispatch, Chronicle, Daily News, Mirror, Globe, Journal, Enquirer, and so forth. Use the dictionary to find out what these names mean. What is the name of your local newspaper? Does your school have a newspaper? What is its name? What do these names mean?

2. How do people receive their daily newspaper? Have the children ask adults they know how they choose to get their newspaper (e.g., home delivery, the stand at the pharmacy, on the Internet). Which means is most popular? Why? Is there a difference in price?

3. Newspapers from around the world can be found on the Internet. Have the children locate newspapers from countries they are studying in social studies. How are these newspapers similar to or different from your local newspaper?

4. Make a bulletin board display of newspapers and newsletters that come to the homes of the students (e.g., a neighborhood newsletter, a service club bulletin, news from the school superintendent).

5. What qualities must young people possess to be successful news carriers? Have the children fill out an application form for becoming a news carrier. Then have them write a letter in which they write out their qualifications for the job. Note: The application is provided in Figure 7.1.

The Downtown Gazette and Chronicle
Est. 1952

News Carrier Application Form

Name: _____

Address: _____

Telephone Number: _____

Grade in school: ___

Availability: _____

References: _____

_____

_____

_____

Figure 7.1. News carrier application form.

6. Imagine that you are a beginning news carrier. Design an announcement card to introduce yourself to your customers. Specify your name, address, and telephone number. Indicate your willingness to honor special requests, for example, saving papers while the customer is on vacation.

7. What are the advantages for a young person having a newspaper route? What are the disadvantages? Would a morning or afternoon route be better? Tally the answers from the class and make a bar graph to explain the answers.

8. Have the children ask their teachers, parents, and grandparents if they were news carriers. What do these adults feel they gained from having the responsibility of a job as a young person? Share the stories with the class.

9. A common reason for being a news carrier is to earn money. Suppose the carrier receives six cents for delivering the daily edition and ten cents for the Sunday edition. How much money will the news carrier earn delivering 50 daily newspapers each week? How much will the carrier earn delivering seventy-five Sunday papers? How much would be earned if 45 papers were delivered for all seven days each week? For 45 papers every day for twenty weeks? Do news carriers have any expenses that must be deducted from their earnings? Note: Money left after any expenses are paid is called a "profit." If there are no expenses, the money earned is all profit.

10. Have a discussion on how news carriers might spend the profit from their route. Are there things they must buy (e.g., clothes, school lunches)? Things they want to buy (e.g., computer games, CDs)? Should they save some? Where? In a bank account? In a piggy bank?

11. What other jobs can be done by young children (e.g., babysitting, walking dogs, cleaning the cellar)? Which jobs are most common? What skills are needed to do these jobs right? How much per hour do the children think they should be paid for these jobs? How old should a child be to do them? If children do these tasks at home, should they be paid for them?

12. Child labor is illegal in the United States but there are special provisions for some kinds of work. Ask the school principal, social worker, or other expert to explain to the class what jobs can be legally done outside the home by young people. Some jobs, such as retail clerk, are covered by special permission papers. Have the visitor explain how this works. Can young children work for parents? Relatives? Neighbors? Others?

13. Word Search

    These are the words in the word search (Figure 7.2, page 46).

News carrier	Sunday	Bicycle
Daily	Edition	News bag
Weekly	Route	Profit

References

Kroeger, Mary Kay. *Paperboy*. Boston: Houghton Mifflin, Clarion Books, 1996.

```
E X Z Y Q H E S A Z N G A T L T D X O Y
G D A I L Y I X D M E D N A Y R T N A X
M G F N U D N R F A N K C A L N Y H R D
E I B X O Y D C O Y C F G U O D P E M G
S D E Y F W N S N U B K M G P L U R D A
U O I E B A T F U N L L B Q S S Z R D L
X Y B T N Z N R Z N E U T D G V K M Z
S M T T I J S I Q J D W N C N V A P E S
D O Z H H O H J K S Z A S D D H N C Q W
K I V X A V N G X T I P Y B V A T B L J
X B R G I W Z R C R V H B C A F I P V V
W B J B P S A O L Q G T R I L G M R M K
R R U M I I N V Y C M R O D C R X O P P
P Y I L W C K G R U P F U W V M U F H S
A N N F E G Y R U P E K T I I G O I C H
L T E J F K M C U S Q P E M R Q D T H C
G Q W L Z U P Y L O R X D U I T M R C E
N E B X N Q L F W E E K L Y G W D Y T X
F G D S P N E W S C A R R I E R V S G F
M E G V S W M C Z K E M F J U H Y J N V
```

1. Delivers newspapers
   __ __ __ __ __ __ __ __ __ __

6. The customary fixed course of travel __ __ __ __ __

2. Published every day __ __ __ __ __ __

7. Special container for carrying newspapers __ __ __ __ __ __ __

3. Published once each week __ __ __ __ __ __

8. Money made after expenses __ __ __ __ __ __

4. The largest newspaper of the week __ __ __ __ __ __ __

9. A two-wheeled means of transportation __ __ __ __ __ __ __

5. All the papers printed on one day __ __ __ __ __ __ __

Figure 7.2. News carrier word search.

CHAPTER 8

So You Want to Be President

Judith St. George
New York: Philomel, 2000

Summary

This book explores the presidency as an example of upper management leadership. It is written as a series of humorous vignettes and tells the stories of the presidents and how each succeeded or failed in his role as president.

Theme

The work of the president is to provide leadership to the country.

Content Related Concepts

Presidency, leadership

Content Related Words

Candidate, election, inauguration, White House, constitution, personality, responsibility, leadership, image

Activities

1. Upper management workers must assume leadership roles as an integral part of their job description. Leaders must know what to do, how to do it, and why it must be done. In small groups have students discuss situations in which there must be leadership (e.g., having a championship basketball team, organizing a food drive, winning the PTA membership banner, collecting money for a children's hospital).

2. Leaders must be able to communicate well. To do this, they need to speak and write in ways that are clear, concise, and convincing. They also need to stick to the topics and defend their positions. Ask the children to practice communication and persuasion skills by explaining what might be done in the following situations, for example: a child is late for school three times in one week, three chorus members cannot attend a dress rehearsal for a concert, two students have petitioned to take sixth grade math in the fifth grade, one class has asked permission to take a field trip to a nearby historical monument.

3. Leaders must be able to read and interpret information critically. This involves the use of many reading skills and abilities (e.g., observing, comparing and contrasting, making inferences, making decisions, predicting, drawing conclusions). Use reading textbooks to find examples of lessons that stress these skills. Have the children make up similar activities after they are familiar with the skills.

4. Leaders must establish and achieve goals. Have each student adopt a goal, work toward it, achieve it, and give a brief report to the class on how it was done (e.g., reading a certain number of books in 5 weeks, passing all tests in all subjects for 10 weeks, raising their math average from 70 percent to 85 percent over 20 weeks, walking two miles per week after 5 weeks, entering the science fair). Can these goals be reached? Must some of them be modified? Note: A goal is something to achieve or obtain according to a predetermined purpose.

5. A good leader is a good decision maker. There are times when students may be called on to make a decision. Have the children decide what they would do next in the following situations, for example: smoke is rising from a building, an automobile crashes into a stop sign, a classmate is seen looking at small pieces of paper during a test, a new student from another country is not being included in recess activities.

6. People in upper management positions have personal power. Look up the definitions of "power" in several dictionaries and write them on the board. Have the children write a paragraph titled, "What is power?" What people do they think have power—teachers, rock stars, sports personalities? How do people get power? How do they lose it?

7. A job description explains what a person does on a day-to-day basis in his or her job. Have the children each write a brief job description (one or two paragraphs) for the U.S. president or other leader (e.g., CEO of a computer company, university president, high ranking military person). Refer to the criteria about leadership given in the examples above. Then have them write one for themselves as students and compare the two descriptions.

8. Have each student write a job description of a leadership position they would like to have someday. What would their responsibilities be? What education would they need? What other experience would be helpful?

9. The president and other leaders must deal with much stress in their lives. Watch TV or read newspapers and magazines to find instances when the president, or other leader, appears stressed. How do leaders deal with stress? Is it possible to overcome it? Look for examples on TV or in media pictures that show these leaders relaxing, for example, golfing, fishing, vacationing at Camp David, and so forth.

10. Divide a bulletin board in half with a line. Label one side, "Good Things About the Presidency." Label the other side, "Bad Things about the Presidency." Throughout the unit, invite students to tack statements, cartoons, poems, stories, or pictures on the bulletin board (e.g., Good—you can raid the kitchen at any time; Bad—you can't ever be alone without the Secret Service).

11. Create another bulletin board that displays the names and pictures of the U.S. presidents. Refer to these during the unit and encourage students to learn to recognize these

people. Do the students recognize those who were president during their lifetime? Reserve a corner of the bulletin board for pictures of other heads of state who are in contact with the U.S. president. Note: The Internet and the daily newspaper are good sources for the pictures.

12. In an election, many people do not vote for the issues. They vote for someone who is handsome or has a nice voice, for example. This is known as voting for someone's "image." Divide the class into groups. Have each group select one member who will receive a "makeover" to create a "winning image." This makeover could include hairstyle, clothing, manner of speaking, campaign promises made, and so forth. Take a vote. Have the students vote on image, not issues. Which candidate wins? Why? Is this the best candidate for the job?

13. People in leadership positions must "dress for success." Why? Ask the children to draw pictures or find some in magazines showing how the president dresses for everyday business and others showing how he dresses for relaxation. When would children need to "dress for success"?

14. Many leaders and other professionals must take an oath, or formally promise, that they will do their job to the best of their ability. This includes the president, legislators, judges, public officials, military personnel, physicians, and so forth. Have the students write an oath or solemn promise of office that their school or class president might use. Note: The oath or solemn promise need not be religious in nature.

15. Make a presidential time line covering the years from 1789 to the present. Place each president's name in the appropriate space along with other important events in American and world history. If possible, hang this in the hall so it can be stretched out fully. Have students find or draw pictures to illustrate events in the different decades.

16. Crossword Puzzle

    These are the words for the crossword puzzle (Figure 8.1, page 50).

Election	Personality	Oath	Image
White House	Responsibility	Candidate	Leadership
Constitution	Inauguration		

References

Adams, Simon. *Presidents of the United States*. Princeton, NJ: Two-Can Publishing, 2001.

Figure 8.1. Presidential crossword puzzle.

ACROSS

5. Ability to guide a group of people

6. A solemn promise

7. One who runs for office

9. A list of written promises to the country

10. Characteristics which make us what we are

DOWN

1. A ceremony to take office

2. How others see you

3. The president's home

4. Things one must do

8. A process for choosing a president

CHAPTER 9

Blueberries for Sal

Robert McCloskey
New York: Viking, 1948

Summary

When Little Sal and her mother went blueberry picking, Little Sal was more interested in investigating the world around her and eating blueberries than in berry picking. Little Bear also had trouble tending to the berry picking and soon the two youngsters were mixed up with each other on Blueberry Hill. Fortunately all was straightened out and each one went home with her own mother.

Theme

People, as well as animals, must work to provide food for the winter. The responsibility of the adult is to care for the child's safety as well as supply food and shelter.

Content Related Concepts

preparation for the winter, food preservation

Content Related Words

blueberries, tin pail, canning, stump, hustle, hibernation

Activities

1. Find out about blueberries. The keywords "blueberries," "Maine Cooperative Extension Service," and "blueberry recipes" will access a number of Web sites about blueberries. Also, check these: info@wildblueberries.com or bberry@blueberry.org.

2. Blueberries are grown in places called "blueberry barrens." Use the illustrations in the book to help describe these areas. In what states are blueberries commercially harvested? Research the topic in the Library Media Center.

3. Little Sal's mother and the mother bear were very serious about finding blueberries. Little Sal's mother planned to preserve them for use during the winter. The bears were going to eat the blueberries now, which would store the food for the winter. Did Little Sal and the bear cub see this trip as work? Or did they think the trip was for pleasure? Are there times when Mom and Dad want to work but the kids want to play? What kind of work can children do to help at home?

4. This story is an example of a parallel plot—two similar events happening at the same time. Do parallel plots ever take place in the classroom? Discuss these. Do the children know of other books that have parallel plots?

5. Both Little Sal and the bear cub were lost on the mountain. Have the children write about a time they got lost, perhaps in a store or at a baseball game. Who found them? How? How did the children feel when they were lost and after they had been found? Have the children illustrate their answers.

6. Little Sal's mother wanted to "can" the blueberries. What did this mean? See the flyleaf of the book to see her doing this in the kitchen. Can someone come to the class to explain the home canning process? Someone from the Cooperative Extension Service may be able to demonstrate this for the class. What items were usually home canned (e.g., tomatoes, beans, peaches)? Why would someone can at home? How would small children be able to help in the kitchen?

7. Little Sal's mother's kitchen looks different from kitchens today. What are the differences? How would the appliances and fixtures be different between an older and a modern kitchen? Have the children design a kitchen of their own using newspaper ads or store sale flyers. Each project should contain a floor plan.

8. Take a trip to the school kitchen. Does it look like Sal's mother's kitchen or like ones in today's homes? Ask the cafeteria director if food for school lunches is preserved or is it fresh? What are the sources of the food? How do cafeteria workers know how much food to prepare for a day? What are the favorite lunches? Graph these favorites.

9. Tasks for young children often are based on counting. Practice "counting blueberries" using the small blue disks or bears that come with sets of math manipulatives. Simple math problems can be performed as well.

10. Simulate the dropping of blueberries into the pail by tossing cotton balls into a pail or plastic bucket. Who can stand the farthest away and still reach the target? Keep track of each person's try and declare a winner.

11. Have the children draw pictures of different scenes in the book. Sequence these on the black board or bulletin board to make a story.

12. Blueberries are packaged in many different ways in the grocery store (e.g., fresh, frozen, dried, canned, in pie fillings, or in baked goods). How much does a package or container of berries cost—(e.g., 16 ounces of blueberry pie filling is $1.99, $2.69 for a pint of fresh berries). What comparisons can be made among the various containers? How do these prices compare to other canned, frozen, or fresh fruit (e.g., apples, applesauce, apple pie filling)? Note: Fresh berries will be more available in late summer and early fall.

13. Using recipes from home or the Internet, bring in food for a blueberry festival. If you visited cafeteria workers for this unit, invite them to this celebration. Children may wish to bring in their special teddy bears. Teachers can join the fun and bring in their own teddy bears. Note: The keywords "blueberry recipes" will access instructions for making many tasty treats along with a lesson plan on blueberries.

14. Most blueberries are picked by hand or with a scoop-like rake. For information on harvesting blueberries, access Merrill Blueberry Farms in Ellsworth, Maine, on the Internet at: http://www.merrillwildblueberries.com.

Figure 9.1. Teddy bear.

15. How much do the children know about real bears? Research this topic in the Library Media Center or on the Internet. How many different kinds of bears are there? How big do they grow? What do they eat? Do they sleep all winter? Are they dangerous to people?

16. Another story of a mother bear and her two cubs is *The Legend of Sleeping Bear*. What other "bear" stories do the children know?

17. Have the library media specialist locate other books by Robert McCloskey, such as *One Morning in Maine* and *Make Way for Ducklings*. Note: Little Sal also appears in the book, *One Morning in Maine*.

18. Working as a group, young children can help make a five-line poem about Sal's trip to pick blueberries. Directions are as follows:

Line one—The topic: a person, place, or thing

Line two—Two words describing the thing in line one

Line three—Three describing words ending in –ing or –ed

Line four—One short line about the topic; a phrase

Line five—A synonym for the topic, or the topic repeated

Here is one example of a five-line poem

Fruit

Round, blue

Picked, dropped, eaten

More in the bushes

Blueberries

19. A different kind of five-line poem may be easier for young children. Make lines one and five identical and tell the topic of the poem. Make lines two, three, and four different lines describing line one. The following is an example:

Bears

Climbing up a hillside

Pausing to eat

Storing food for the winter

Bears

References

Martin, Bill. *Brown Bear, Brown Bear, What Do You See?* New York: Henry Holt, 1992.

McCloskey, Robert. *Make Way for Ducklings*. New York: Viking, 1941.

———— . *One Morning in Maine*. New York: Viking, 1952.

Rosen, Michael. *We're Going on a Bear Hunt*. New York: Simon & Schuster, 1997.

Wargin, Kathy-Jo. *The Legend of Sleeping Bear*. Chelsea, MI: Sleeping Bear Press, 1998.

CHAPTER 10

Lilly's Purple Plastic Purse

Kevin Henkes

New York: Greenwillow Books, 1996

Summary

Lilly thought Mr. Slinger was the best teacher in the world. But when he scolded her for bringing a purple plastic purse to class, she changed her mind. She did her best to show how angry she was, until Mr. Slinger told her that today had been a bad day and promised tomorrow would be better.

Theme

The job of a teacher involves skillfully addressing the needs of the individual as well as the group.

Content Related Concepts

educational setting, sharing

Content Related Words

privacy, considerate, uncooperative, encyclopedias, performance, interpretive

Activities

1. Lilly thought Mr. Slinger was a wonderful teacher because he said "Howdy" instead of "Good Morning, Pupils." What other reasons did she have for liking Mr. Slinger, for example, did he let her clap the erasers?

2. Have the children write down what they think makes a teacher special. They can choose characteristics of any of the teachers they know. Select the top 10 reasons and make a poster or computer graphic to be mounted on the bulletin board. Then brainstorm the characteristics that make a student special, for example, he or she always raises their hand. Add these to the bulletin board. Graphics can be obtained from a clip art program to illustrate this project.

3. How do adults judge the effectiveness of a teacher (e.g., they work well with children, they are able to cope with unexpected problems, they institute creative ideas like the Lightbulb Lab)? Ask the principal to give a short presentation on what he or she expects from teachers. Note: Many teachers are given "good teacher awards" from various local, regional, state, and national organizations. How are these teachers chosen? If any winners live nearby, have the students correspond with them about their award.

4. Workers are judged on how well they do their jobs. Have the students list ways of judging whether these people are doing a good job: bus driver, singer, dairy farmer, sports figure, plumber, computer programmer, truck driver, day care provider, construction worker, doctor, grocery store clerk, chef. Note: Familiar occupations chosen by children's parents may be substituted.

5. Good workers are skilled at their jobs, creative, and have the desire to do well. Design a "good worker award" to be given to students when they have a special day. The reward does not have to be given only for academic achievement, but can be awarded for any outstanding act in or around the school. How will the award winners be chosen? Have students help set up criteria for selection and design a "badge of honor" to be presented with it.

Figure 10.1. Good job ribbon.

6.   Lilly had a problem with the whole class when she refused to cooperate. Have the class debate what discipline they feel Lilly should receive if she interrupted their sharing time.

7.   Set up hypothetical examples of other problems that may occur in the classroom (e.g., taking food or money from other children, failing to bring in homework, damaging classroom materials or equipment). Note: Teachers can suggest many topics for discussion by the whole group or small groups.

8.   Mr. Slinger was Lilly's role model. What is a role model? Have the students look up the definition. Who do the students wish to be like? Note: The teacher should set ground rules that a role model be a positive force in a child's life.

9.   Lilly brought in snacks for the classroom. Use the following data to make a bar graph showing the choices of the children in this imaginary classroom.

Fruit, 3 students   Corn chips, 2 students

Cookies, 5 students   Vegetables, 3 students

Twinkies, 4 students   Cheese and crackers, 4 students

Rank the snacks from best to least liked. Which would be considered to be "healthy snacks"? What is the value of using a graph to visualize this?

10.   Compare the above chart to one made after asking the students about their favorite snacks.

11.   In an acrostic, the letters of a word are written top to bottom. Each letter begins a word to describe the topic. Here is an acrostic for "teacher." Have the children try another example using other names or topics from the story, for example, student or school bus.

Tremendous

Exceptional

Amazing

Cheerful

Happy

Exciting

Resourceful

12.   In the story, the class shared many books as they learned from Mr. Slinger. Pretend that the teacher has received $500 to buy new books for the classroom library. Have each student recommend the title of a book or a topic they would like to read about. Subtract $16 (the average cost of a children's hard bound book) for each book selected. Keep making selections until all the money is spent. Approximately how many books can be bought? Note: Teachers may have publisher's catalogues available to introduce new literature to the students. Or there may be a source, such as a local bookstore, where a discount might be applied to any real orders.

13. Word Search

These are the words in the word search (Figure 10.2, page 59).

Mr. Slinger	Sharing time	Snacks	Desk
School	Book	Purse	Recess
Bus	Lightbulb Lab	Lunchroom	Necktie

References

Thaler, Mike. *The Teacher from the Black Lagoon*. New York: Econo-Clad Books, 1999.

Weiss, Leatie. *My Teacher Sleeps in School*. New York: Viking, 1985.

```
X  H  M  H  J  L  Q  T  G  W  A  J  F  R  N  I  T  I  L  D
R  Y  R  D  M  C  O  E  Q  N  C  L  K  L  E  D  U  W  I  Y
Y  H  S  V  T  H  V  N  A  L  L  R  N  E  X  D  Y  B  G  O
T  X  L  I  X  E  S  S  I  L  A  W  D  V  L  L  N  X  H  W
E  U  I  Z  T  U  C  A  L  S  M  V  E  B  C  U  E  T  T  I
F  L  N  S  N  F  E  X  E  P  W  W  S  U  E  N  C  B  B  K
F  T  G  N  K  G  Y  R  S  R  C  F  K  S  T  C  K  J  U  G
Y  I  E  A  C  Q  S  I  B  O  O  K  I  U  F  H  T  B  L  S
N  E  R  C  L  Z  M  B  B  C  M  K  U  N  K  R  I  W  B  K
L  A  T  K  I  X  Z  Q  X  Y  Y  X  X  U  J  O  E  T  L  L
H  Z  R  S  G  K  F  C  D  G  R  C  F  T  G  O  Q  D  A  C
U  U  M  H  Q  O  P  D  T  Q  J  C  M  M  K  M  U  E  B  Z
P  W  K  A  W  F  D  E  R  F  F  X  I  F  U  K  I  H  Q  N
H  P  U  R  S  E  C  W  E  K  C  C  Z  L  D  C  W  G  Z  V
Q  D  S  T  V  O  T  S  C  H  O  O  L  T  N  O  S  D  G  J
W  G  D  G  K  T  G  T  E  S  E  O  S  J  T  N  H  C  M  S
P  X  N  H  I  X  L  X  S  M  U  P  P  B  E  X  K  Y  A  N
H  F  Z  A  U  R  F  V  S  N  I  A  L  A  H  G  O  T  T  Y
S  S  H  A  R  I  N  G  T  I  M  E  Q  A  E  T  M  C  P  B
O  M  F  W  H  Y  D  H  Y  R  M  R  W  O  A  B  P  F  E
```

1. A favorite teacher __ __ __ __ __ __ __ __ __

2. A place to learn __ __ __ __ __ __ __

3. A vehicle to ride to school __ __ __

4. Telling about yourself __ __ __ __ __ __ __ __ __ __ __

5. It can be read for pleasure __ __ __ __

6. A place to go when your work is done __ __ __ __ __ __ __ __ __ __ __

7. Treats of food __ __ __ __ __ __

8. It was purple and made of plastic __ __ __ __ __ __

9. A place to eat __ __ __ __ __ __ __ __ __ __

10. Each child's own seat __ __ __ __ __

11. Time to take a break __ __ __ __ __ __ __

12. Mr. Slinger wore this around his neck __ __ __ __ __ __ __

Figure 10.2. Lilly's word search.

CHAPTER 11

A New Coat for Anna

Harriet Ziefert
New York: Alfred A. Knopf, 1986

Summary

After the war, there were few items to buy and little money with which to buy them. Anna's mother used her bartering skills to get the items to make a new coat for her daughter.

Theme

A variety of special skills are needed to make a superior product in an economy that is based on trading goods and services.

Content Related Concepts

handmade, mass production, assembly line, barter economy

Content Related Words

lingonberry, shear, porcelain, tailor, garnet, measurements

Activities

1. Discussing the topic of war will help build background knowledge for Anna's story, which takes place after a war. Ask children for their answers to the statement, "War is when . . . " Record their comments on the board as a preview to discussing the question, "What is war?" It might be helpful to also record their answers to the question, "What is peace?"

2. Look at the first picture in the book. This shows Anna's homeland after it had been devastated by war—perhaps World War II. What observations about Anna's life can the children make by looking at this picture? Are there still places in the world where war has caused great destruction? Discuss them.

3. Anna probably lived in northern Europe (e.g., Scandinavia, Belgium, the Netherlands, England, Germany, or Poland). Locate these countries on a classroom map of the world or on a globe. Also find areas where wars have taken place recently, for example, Eastern Europe, the Middle East, and Africa.

4. Have the children make a list of essential facilities that would need to be rebuilt after a war. For example, hospitals and food stores would be urgently needed, but movie theaters might be considered a luxury for a while.

5. Anna needed a new coat but her mother could not afford to buy her one. What circumstances kept them from buying a coat? Does this compare to the situation when students need the next size coat? Where can we find coats and jackets to buy today—discount stores, thrift shops, mail order catalogues, and department stores? To practice purchasing a coat, students can select coats from a mail order catalog and write up a pretend order.

6. To get a coat for Anna, her mother had to trade precious items for goods and services with, for example, the sheep farmer, the spinner, the weaver, and the tailor. When people trade items for goods or services it is called a "barter economy." This type of trade still takes place in many parts of the world. Have the children ever traded one thing for another (e.g., lunch items, baseball cards, comics). Why did they do it? Why is barter seldom used in the United States today? Note: A flow chart can be used to show the process of making Anna's coat, from shearing the sheep to sewing the coat together (Figure 11.1).

7. Ask the children to think of their most precious possession. Would they ever trade it? Under what circumstances and how would they feel?

8. All of the craftsmen in the story were very skilled at their trades. Are there similar craftspeople in your town who could give a lecture or demonstration to the class? Find other craftspeople as well, such as woodworkers, potters, and painters. Note: Get names of people from a local arts council, from a craft store, from an art teacher, or by advertising in the newspaper.

9. Mother and Anna gathered lingonberries. Why did mother use this fruit to dye the yarn? Are there other dyes that come from natural products (e.g., onion skins, nuts, beet juice, berries, red cabbage)? Experiment with dyeing using these items and small pieces of white cloth. Does the color remain after the cloth is washed? Note: Teachers should boil berries, cabbage, or whatever is used, for a few minutes, and then drain the liquid into jars to cool. Under supervision, children may dunk swatches of cloth into each color. Swatches may be held with clothespins so that fingers are not discolored. Have an adult help rinse the swatches and lay them out to dry. Compare the colors.

10. Lingonberries are native to northern Europe. How are lingonberries used? Learn more about these berries by accessing this Web site: http://www.lingonberries.com. Note: It may be possible to buy lingonberry preserves in your area at a gourmet or specialty store. If so, give each student a taste. What do they think of it?

11. Is it possible to get a tailor-made coat or suit in this country today? Check the yellow pages of the phone book for tailors. What other tasks do tailors do?

12. Gather some leftover sewing items that tailors would have (e.g., buttons, ribbons, felt, cloth scraps). Attach these to pieces of cardboard to make wall hangings or paste them onto fabric and clothing. A collection of items inside a glass jar is also an attractive way to display sewing notions such as buttons. Note: Parents who sew or do crafts may be able to donate scraps to the class.

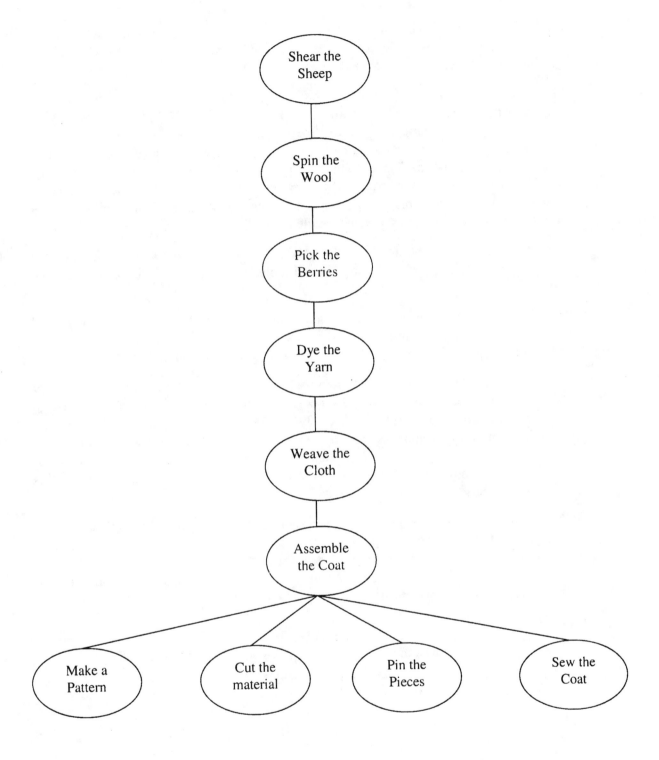

Figure 11.1. Anna's coat flow chart.

13. Have each child design a coat for Anna. Cut the coat out of fabric, construction paper, wallpaper samples, and so forth. Add buttons and trim. Note: Catalog pictures can be used to get ideas for coats.

14. Anna's coat was made from wool, which provides the most warmth for the wearer. To see why this is, examine wool yarn with a magnifying glass. Notice that the yarn is not smooth and symmetrical. It has little fibers, which shoot off the strand and capture tiny pockets of air to form an insulation layer. Acrylic yarns will not have these fibers sticking out of the strand. Therefore, they do not trap layers of air and there is little insulation. Note: Natural wool fibers coated with animal oils also insulate against the cold when they are wet. This does not happen with man-made fibers. Some children might be allergic to wool and shouldn't handle it directly.

15. Wrap similar ice cubes in identically sized pieces of wool and acrylic. Which ice cube is slower melting? Why? Repeat this with pieces of various fabrics and discuss the results.

16. The dedication of the book is to the lady who was the real Anna. What is her job now? Why do students think she kept the coat? How do they think she feels about her mother? What questions would students ask her if they could meet her?

17. As part of the millenium celebration in 2000, many books on the twentieth century were compiled. Using one of these books from the Library Media Center, study the years dedicated to World War II (1939–1945). The postwar years (1945–the early 1950s) may also be included because many events during that time were related to the war, for example, the Berlin Airlift and the rebuilding of Europe. Make a time line of important events of that era. Note: The story of Anna would take place during this postwar period.

18. To wrap up the unit, hold a jacket and coat drive for local people who need them. Items can be dropped off at the school and picked up by an organization, such as a church group or service club, which will distribute them. Note: Consider rewarding the homeroom that collects the greatest number of coats with a treat, for example, a pizza lunch or an extra gym class.

19. Crossword Puzzle

    These are the words for the crossword puzzle (Figure 11.2, page 65).

Weaver	Lingonberries	Tailor	Barter
Yarn	Teapot	Garnet	Wool
Farmer	Spinner		

References

Duvall, Jill. *Ms. Moja Makes Beautiful Clothes*. New York: Children's Press, 1997.

Jennings, Peter, and Todd Brewster. *The Century for Young People*. New York: Random House (A Doubleday Book for Young Readers), 1999.

ACROSS

1. He fits and sews the clothing
3. Fabric made from the fleece of a sheep
5. To trade one item for another
6. A person who makes wool into yarn
8. A semi-precious gem or stone
9. Raises sheep and lambs

Down

2. Similar in taste and appearance to cranberries
3. Uses a loom to make fabric
4. The final thing traded to the tailor
7. A continuous strand of twisted fibers

Figure 11.2. Anna's coat crossword puzzle.

CHAPTER 12

Working Cotton

Sherley Anne Williams
San Diego: Harcourt Brace Jovanovich, 1992

Summary

Shelan was not old enough to have her own bag for picking cotton like her older sisters. All she could do was pile cotton in the middle of the row for Mamma and watch the baby. It was hard work for everyone, but Daddy and his family were proud of the good job they did. Shelan dreamed of a day when she, too, would be able to have a sack of her own to help the family.

Theme

A skillful worker takes great pride in his or her accomplishments. There is a dignity to work.

Content Related Concepts

migrant workers, foreign born

Content Related Words

itinerant, weighing device, sack, greens, humanitarian

Activities

1. To get up-to-date materials on migrant workers on the Internet, use the keywords "migrant worker." Or use the website http://www.eiu.edu/

2. Who are migrant workers? Where do they live? Where do they usually work? What is the importance of the migrant worker to the economy of a given area?

3. List the problems of the migrant family, using one column for the father, one for the mother, and one for the children. For example, the father may not be able to speak English or cannot save any money to buy a home for his family; the mother knows that there is no health insurance when the children are sick; the children change schools so often that they never get to master the subjects and they don't stay in one place long enough to make friends. Note: Use information from the Internet to expand on these reasons.

4. Other problems of the migrant worker include low wages, long days in the fields, hot weather, little water to drink while working, unsanitary conditions, poor housing, discrimination, exposure to pesticides, fear of reprisals for joining organizations that fight for workers' rights, and so forth. How would these conditions affect the educational and social lives of the migrant children? Note: Positive aspects of the lives of migrant workers and families should also be stressed (e.g., the strong family structure). Care should be taken so migrant children do not feel inferior.

5. Compare these working conditions to those of the parents of the students in the class. Simple terms such as "similar," "different," and "no opinion" could be used. Note: This should not be occasion to complain about jobs and management, but rather a chance to seriously compare the plight of the migrant worker to the average American worker.

6. Many programs have been formed to help migrant children. For example, the Penn State College Assistance Program offers testing and tutoring of children to help them pick up academic skills, to learn to speak English, and to become acquainted with other students. Are there other programs of assistance in the students' community? If they could help create a new program, what aspects might it entail?

7. There are about 700,000 migrant workers in the United States—far more than the population of Washington, DC. If all of these workers assembled in one area, how would their population compare to the size of the students' community? To their state's? Of these workers, 90 percent are foreign born. What does this term mean? Identify the countries from which workers come. Note: See Internet sources recommended in number 1 for recent information.

8. One city that depends heavily on migrant workers for the labor supply is Fresno, California, the center of a large agricultural area. Locate Fresno on the map of the United States. Using *The World Almanac*, find climatological data about rainfall, average monthly temperature, high temperature, low temperature, number of days clear and cloudy, and air quality, as well as any other information that seems interesting about Fresno. Compare these findings to the weather that Shelan experienced in the book. What would life be like living in the Fresno area? Note: There is an outline map of the United States in Chapter 2, *Potato: A Tale of the Great Depression*.

9. In the book, Shelan says, "It's a long time to night." What does this mean? Compare a typical day for Shelan with that of the children in class (e.g., What does Shelan do to help the family? How long is her day? What food do they have during the day? Do the children go to school? When she goes "home," what does it really mean? How would she like things to be different?).

10. What one small piece of beauty does Shelan find during her day? Have the children draw a picture of something they think is truly a beautiful part of their day.

Figure 12.1. Cotton plant.

11. Cotton does not weigh very much. To buy cotton in the drugstore, you would find boxes containing two ounces or four ounces. How many two-ounce boxes of cotton would be needed to make a 50-pound bale? A 100-pound bale? A 200-pound bale? How many four-ounce boxes? How much space would the cotton take up? Note: Cotton balls are measured by number, not by weight, and cannot be used for comparison purposes.

12. Cotton is very absorbent and can hold great quantities of water. Place a few cotton balls in a plastic cup and saturate them with water. Squeeze out the excess water. Put 2 or 3 bean seeds in the middle of the cotton and place the cup on a windowsill. Keep the cotton moist. How long does it take for the bean to sprout? Where did the energy to sprout the bean come from? Can the bean continue to grow in this medium?

13. Teachers may wish to introduce information on the history of the cotton industry. This would include topics such as slavery, the plantation system, the industrial revolution, and the invention of the cotton gin. Modern methods of production have changed the cotton industry of today. What types of jobs are involved in the growth and harvesting of cotton? Research answers using library resources or the Internet.

14. The young boy in *Tomas and the Library Lady* (Chapter 13) is also the son of migrant workers. How is Tomas' life different from Shelan's? Have the children write a reaction to the lives of the two children and compare it to their own way of life.

15. Another story of a migrant worker child in California is *Blue Willow* by Doris Gates. This book could be read chapter by chapter throughout the unit. Have the children compare the lives and dreams of the main characters in the two books.

16. Ask the library media specialist to find information on two activists who helped the migrant workers' cause—for example, Cesar Chavez and Dolores Huerta. What were their backgrounds? Why did they want to help others? What did they do to aid the migrant workers of America? What problems did they have to face as they tried to accomplish their goals? Have the children decide why these people might be candidates for a humanitarian award.

17. Find the letter that corresponds to each number. Use these numbers to fill in the blanks. This should spell out a line from the book. Note: Further instructions for math puzzles are found in Chapter 6, *Waiting for the Evening Star*.

A	B	C	D	E	F	G	H	I	J	K	L	M
1	2	3	4	5	6	7	8	9	10	11	12	13

N	O	P	Q	R	S	T	U	V	W	X	Y	Z
14	15	16	17	18	19	20	21	22	23	24	25	26

9 20 19 ___ 1 ___ 12 15 14 7 ___ 20 9 13 5

___ ___ ___   ___   ___ ___ ___ ___   ___ ___ ___ ___

        20 15 ___ 14 9 7 8 20

        ___ ___   ___ ___ ___ ___ ___

18. Another resource for the teacher to share with the students is *Voices from the Fields*, by S. Beth Atkin. What topics do the students in the book share? What are their dreams? How could their lives enrich the lives of other students?

19. Well-written books can be valuable resources for learning about people of diverse cultures. After reading *Working Cotton*, have the class answer and discuss the following questions about the book. Use these criteria to judge other multicultural books such as

Tomas and the Library Lady. Note: The library media specialist should have a selection of multicultural works from which to choose.

- Is the story historically and culturally correct?

- Are the characters treated as individuals and not just part of a group?

- Does the book tell of the feelings and accomplishments of the individual?

- Are problems realistically faced? Are solutions practical?

- Is diversity in the culture positively recognized?

- Are terms or illustrations used that are degrading to the individuals?

- Does the book have a strong plot, setting, characterization, and theme? Are there values worth imparting to the reader?

NOTE: This may be an appropriate place to introduce the word "stereotype"—the unwarranted discrimination against persons based on race, color, religion, ethnic background, sexual preference, physical impairment, etc.

References

Atkin, S. Beth. *Voices from the Fields: Children of Migrant Workers Tell Their Stories*. Boston: Little, Brown, 1993.

Gates, Doris. *Blue Willow*. New York: Viking, 1940.

Mora, Pat. *Tomas and the Library Lady*. New York: Alfred A. Knopf, 1997.

CHAPTER 13

Tomas and the Library Lady

Pat Mora
New York: Alfred A. Knopf, 1997

Summary

Tomas was the child of migrant workers who lived part of the year in Iowa and part in Texas. Tomas missed his own house and his own bed when they were in Iowa, but it was here that he found the public library and the library lady. She helped him find books of interest and arranged for him to take books home. Even Papa Grande, the family storyteller, was impressed by the stories Tomas could now tell. This love of books was so strong that Tomas would someday become a librarian helping others.

Theme

A trained professional demonstrates her skill by providing nurturing literature for developing minds. People also need role models to mentor them.

Content Related Concepts

migrant worker, storytelling

Content Related Words

buenas noches, en un tiempo pasado, uno, dos, thre, cuarto, qué tigre tan grande, libro, pájaro, buenos tardes, señor, adiós, pan dulce, gracias

Activities

1. For further information on the life of migrant workers see Chapter 12, *Working Cotton*, which lists Internet sources and other titles.

2. Tomas lives in Iowa for part of the year and Texas for the other part. Locate these two states on a map of the United States. Note: There is an outline map of the United States in Chapter 2, *Potato: A Tale of the Great Depression*.

3. Plan a motor trip between the two states: What is the best route to follow? Are these secondary or super highways? How many miles is the trip? If a car gets 20 miles to the gallon and gas is two dollars a gallon, what would be the cost of gasoline for the trip? How many nights in a motel would the family need to spend? Is it possible to drive straight through from Iowa to Texas? Note: For the purpose of calculating the mileage, use the capital cities of the two states—Des Moines, Iowa, and Austin, Texas. A route can be planned on the Internet using Mapquest.com.

4. Tomas was lucky to live in only two places so that he was able to attend school regularly. Many children of migrant workers go to several schools during a year, and some cannot attend at all. What difference would it make to Tomas if he had to attend many different schools? Students may wish to share their own experiences with being the "new student" in the class.

5. Tomas did not have his own library card, perhaps because he was not a permanent resident of the town. How was he able to take books home? How did this make him feel?

6. Have the children visit the town library and apply for their own library card. Is there a fee? What privileges does the card give to the child? What responsibilities (e.g., a two-week loan period for children's books)?

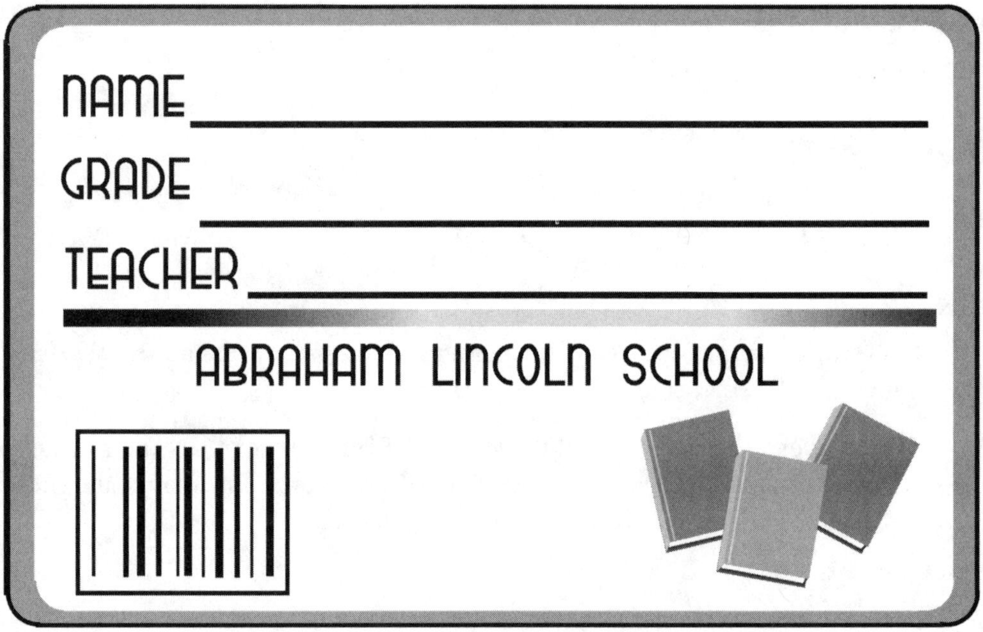

Figure 13.1. Example of a school library card.

7. Have the students imagine that the local library is to be renovated and new technological features will be installed. What should be located on the main floor of the building? Will there be additional floors? What will they house? Have the children design a library floor plan complete with furniture, computers, bookshelves, diskette storage, and the like. Include a floor plan of sections found on other floors (e.g., children's books, historical archives) See figure 13.2, page 76.

8. How long must someone go to college before he or she is able to assume the directorship of a library? What degree do they receive? These are some of the classes that students must take in college to be a librarian. How would they be of help?

   • Introduction to the Library Media Center

   • Selecting Material for the Library Media Center

   • Media for Children and Adolescents

   • Administering the Library Media Center

   • Computers in the Library Media Center

9. The work of the librarian is aided by the work of other degreed and non-degreed workers (e.g., researchers, story hour personnel, archivists, persons who shelve books and read the stacks, custodial staff). Are volunteers used at the library? Student helpers? Ask a librarian.

10. Invite a librarian for a class visit or make a trip to the school or local public library. Have the children write questions to ask: How has the role of the librarian changed over the past 25 years? How do they decide what materials to buy? Are they computer experts? Where do they get money to buy books and other materials? What advice does the librarian have for students interested in this field?

11. Discuss the operation of the school library. How do students find the books and materials they want? Are there nonbook sources found in the library? What jobs does the librarian have besides helping to find books? Do volunteers help in the library?

12. Discuss the basic rules for borrowing books in the school library, the community library, and the classroom library. Why would the rules be different among the three places? Does each library have its own unique rules?

13. Owning a book gives us a very special feeling. Why? Do the students own a favorite book? Discuss ways to acquire books (e.g., bookstores, school-sponsored book clubs, garage sales, second hand bookstores, trading books). Students may wish to donate books they no longer use to the classroom library or to organizations that will ship them to schools in underdeveloped areas. Or arrange a time for students to trade books.

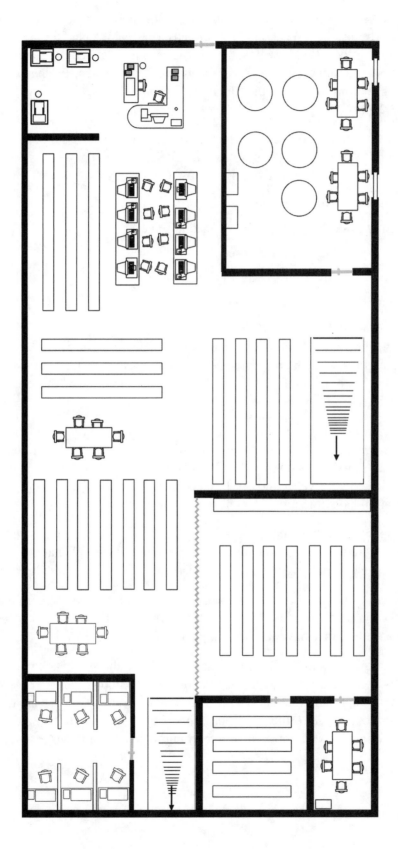

Figure 13.2. Library floor plan.

14. While the class is discussing *Tomas and the Library Lady*, children may wish to adopt or find out what their names would be in Spanish. Boys' first names might include Juan, Jose, Pedro, Carlos, Jorge, Ernesto, Alberto, Miguel, Raoul, Antonio, Jaime, Luis, and Marcos. Girls' first names might include Maria, Josefina, Marta, Herlinda, Antonia, Anita, Juanita, Julia, Ana, Margarita, Teresa, Cristina, and Silvia. Other books portraying the Hispanic culture may also be shared at this time.

15. Tomas wants to be able to tell stories like his grandfather. What exactly is storytelling? How does it differ from just talking? What are some stories that everyone knows—*The Gingerbread Man*, *The Three Little Pigs*, *Paul Bunyan*? Have the children tell stories to the class. Set up guidelines for the length of story, content, purpose, main idea and details, theme or moral.

16. Tomas loved to read and learn. Ask the teachers in your school to write a few lines about how reading helped them to achieve their goals. Share these thoughts on a bulletin board display.

17. Educators agree that one of the best things that parents or older people can do for children is to read to them. In this way, the child learns the vocabulary in the book and hears how language is composed. Ask children to name a special book and tell what they learned from it. Note: This may be a book read in school because all children do not have someone to read to them.

18. Have the children volunteer to read to younger children at home or in school. Share the comments from the younger children. Did he or she enjoy the book? Have the reader write a paragraph describing what it is like to work with a younger child and what they gained from the experience.

19. Reading is necessary for any career. Why? How can students improve their reading? Note: Reading must be practiced like any other skill. Increased vocabulary and problem-solving techniques can enhance reading. Do the children learn a specific list of vocabulary words each week? What subjects are good sources of problem solving?

20. Make a list of book categories and have the children vote for their favorites. The list might include adventure, mystery, romance, westerns, horror, biography, fantasy, animals, and family. Add other categories if desired. Make a graph showing the distribution of the books. Note: Children may wish to select more than one.

21. Survey the class to find out who the children's favorite authors are. Select the top 8 or 10 choices and put these on a graph. Students may wish to write a class letter to the author who is the number one choice. Addresses can be found in the *Something About the Author* or *Contemporary Authors* series. Mail can also be sent to the publisher. Read some of these authors' books together as a group.

22. Have the children design a book cover for one of their favorite books—preferably one that does not already have a paper dust cover. Include a synopsis of the book on the left side flap and information about the author on the right side.

23. Crossword Puzzle

These are the words for the crossword puzzle (Figure 13.3, page 79).

Adios	Storyteller	Migrants	Spanish
Texas	Dinosaurs	Librarians	Vegetables
Iowa			

References

Harrison, James, and Eleanor Van Zandt. *The Young People's Atlas of the United States.* New York: Kingfisher, 1992.

Nakamura, Joyce (managing editor). *Something About the Author.* Farmington Hills, MI: Gale Group, 2000 (current volume)

Peacock, Scot (managing editor). *Contemporary Authors.* Farmington Hills, MI: Gale Group, 2000 (current volume)

Spinelli, Jerry. *The Library Card.* New York: Scholastic, 1997.

Figure 13.3. Tomas's crossword puzzle.

ACROSS

4. Workers who move from job to job

5. They help you to select books

6. One who creates narratives for enjoyment

9. Spanish for goodbye

DOWN

1. In the library Tomas read about these creatures

2. These were picked by the workers

3. The family spoke this language at home

7. A Southern state where Tomas lived

8. The family worked here part of the year

CHAPTER 14

Mommy's Office

Barbara Shook Hazen
New York: Atheneum, 1992

Summary

Emily was thrilled to visit Mommy's office and find that many things were similar to her own "office" at school (e.g., the desk and chair, piles of papers, paperwork to do). Even the coffee break reminded Emily of snack time. After lunch, Mommy's presentation made Emily think of show-and-tell. On the bus ride home, she named all of the things she liked. But Emily thought the best part of the day was seeing how many tasks she and Mommy shared.

Theme

The skills developed by children in school often parallel the job skills of workers in an office.

Content Related Concepts

office work

Content Related Words

office, cafeteria, receptionist, presentation, copy machine, fax machine, coffee break, computers

Activities

1. Ask the children where their parents work (e.g., an office, a factory, a store, a school, a farm). How many different places are represented? Are any of these jobs agricultural? Industrial? Do others fall into the category of information and technology? Where would Mommy's job fit?

2. On a local map, locate the geographical areas where parents work. Do the occupations cluster together, for example, factories in one part of town, stores in another? Perhaps a parent volunteer could take pictures showing several of the places where the parents work. Identify and arrange these for a bulletin board display.

3. Have the children give a brief statement to identify their parents' jobs. Be sure to include mothers and fathers, as well as any other caregivers. Note: If parents are unemployed, have students give the job the parent would like to pursue.

4. With the help of the guidance counselor or library media specialist, Activity 3 can be expanded into a Career Day event. Ask parents to visit and talk about their jobs. Have the students research jobs that interest them and make posters describing jobs they might enjoy. To extend even further, students might shadow persons who are employed in fields of their interest or interview persons in the workplace. Note: The purpose of these activities is to introduce children to a cross-section of occupations. Adults should describe the working conditions of their jobs, educational requirements to enter these jobs, responsibilities they assume, expected income, and so forth. A guidance teacher would have expertise in organizing a Career Day. More information on career activities can found in Chapter 23, *Worksong*.

5. The setting of this book is the office. What is it that defines the word "office"? What offices do the children know (e.g., the principal, the nurse, the doctor, the dentist, the unemployment agency)?

6. Arrange to take a tour of the school offices. Who works there? What is the purpose of their work? What equipment and supplies are found there? Do students or parents volunteer there?

7. Some of the most important persons in any office are the secretaries and administrative assistants. They are responsible for keeping it running smoothly (e.g., arranging appointments, preparing materials, communicating with outside persons). Have one of the school secretaries talk about her job. How was she trained? Has she worked other places? What qualities does she possess (e.g., organizational skills, knowledge of various computer systems)? What does she like about working in a school office? Are secretarial positions still held primarily by women?

8. The job of secretary has changed much in the last several years as the responsibilities have grown and managers have taken on many of the former tasks of their secretaries. New titles reflect their responsibilities (e.g., administrative assistant, office manager, office assistant, management technician). Could some moms or dads give a job description for people who work in these jobs at their place of employment?

9. Perhaps a trip to a large office can be arranged for the class. Before going, give the children an introduction to that office. A member of the office staff should be available to answer questions. Note: Parental permission should be secured for each child making the trip.

10. One of the events Emily saw during the day was her mother's presentation. This is very much like a teacher presenting a lesson. Discuss a lesson that the teacher has given. What is the purpose of the presentation? How do teachers prepare what they are going to say? How do they keep the students' attention? How do they know if the lesson was understood? How do teachers evaluate their lessons?

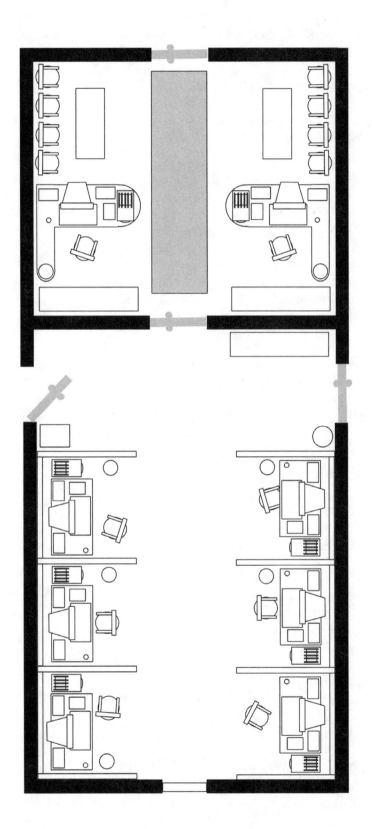

Figure 14.1. Office floor plan.

11. Making a presentation was an important part of Mommy's day. She had spent many hours preparing for it. Have the children work in groups to create a presentation to give to the class on any topic. Here are a few ideas for science presentations:

- Animals that live in societies
- How people and animals change as they grow
- The water cycle
- Preparing for nature's storms
- How we use machines
- Keeping in shape physically

Note: Presentation topics can also be selected to give children a chance to research various subjects using the Library Media Center or the Internet.

12. Have the teacher judge the presentations using the following scale: 5-outstanding, 4-excellent, 3-good, 2-average, and 1-poor. Areas to be considered are content, organization, ability to communicate, and general effectiveness. Use the following chart for evaluating the presentations:

Group Name _____ Teacher's Name_____ Total Score___

Score Points	Content	Organization	Communication	Effectiveness
5				
4				
3				
2				
1				

13. The computer system is of prime importance to any office. What hardware/software does the office use? Who is in charge of the system? What role does the computer play in the work? How many of the office workers use a computer as part of their workday? What happens when the computer is "down"?

14. In the yellow pages, look up "office supply stores." What is the difference between the large nationally-based supply store and a small family-owned office supply store? What are the advantages and disadvantages of each? How do they solicit business from the public? Do they supply catalogs to customers?

15. An office supply store is a very interesting place to visit and see various office equipment and supplies (e.g., copy machines, computers, notebooks and paper, art supplies, office furniture). What hours is the store open? Do the clerks need any special training? What goods are most commonly sold? For more information on office goods that can be found on the Internet, contact this Web site: http://www.henryhall.com

16. Using the information found in Activities 14 and 15, have each child design his or her own office. What will be the purpose of the office? How many employees will be there? Arrange to have a desk for each employee, along with other supplies (e.g., computers, phones, filing cabinets, fax machines).

17. Several years ago, many schools adopted the tradition of setting aside a day on which daughters could go to observe their mother's workplace. This is sometimes called "shadowing" and is an important component of career education. Community members may volunteer to have students shadow them to learn about their jobs. Ask the children for written reflections or oral reports on what they learned by "shadowing" an adult. These can be used to create a bulletin board display along with drawings of themselves in the profession they "shadowed."

18. Finding a job is a large task and everyone needs a resume. Have each child make up a resume for a future job. It should include name, address, phone number, schooling, accomplishments (e.g., chocolate chip cookie baker, neighborhood Nintendo champ, expert skateboarder, American Red Cross babysitting course graduate). What job would they like to pursue? How will their accomplishments help them to carry out this job?

19. An interview is usually part of applying for a job. Conduct a mock interview for students who would like to become a student council member, a crossing guard, a guidance office helper, and so forth. Concentrate on questions that will show the person's ability, not just their popularity.

20. Have students exchange resumes, then interview each other for the job they have chosen. This should be a job they wish to pursue in the future.

21. Some of the important factors to consider in accepting a job offer are salary, benefits, transportation, and day care for young children. Does the firm pay health benefits? Is there public transportation in the area? Are there places that offer their own day care facilities for the employees' children? What other sources of day care can be found?

22. Throughout their working years, people should save for their retirement. Ask a retired member of the community to answer these questions: What is retirement? What do retired people do now that they don't have to go to their jobs? What is the best part of being retired? Are there any problems?

23. Crossword Puzzle

    These are the words for the crossword puzzle (Figure 14.2, page 86).

Pencil sharpener	Keyboard	Desk	Coffee pot
Paper clip	Telephone	Swivel chairs	Microwave
Printer	File folders	Calendar	Staple
Paper	Copy machine	Wastebasket	

References

Waber, Bernard. *Lyle at the Office*. Boston: Houghton Mifflin, 1996.

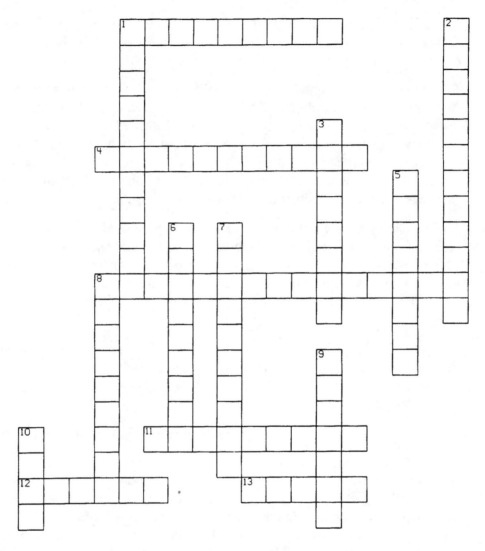

ACROSS

1. An electrical device for making drinks

4. A small trash receptacle

8. A device needed to put a point on a pencil

11. A device to transmit voices over a wire

12. A small metal fastener for holding papers together

13. Writing material made from wood pulp

DOWN

1. It reproduces written material

2. Furniture to sit upon

3. A device to input letters and numbers into the computer

5. A listing of dates for the year

6. A heating device for foods or water

7. Folded cardboard used to hold pages together

8. A reusable metal paper holder

9. It produces images from a computer

10. Furniture used to write upon

Figure 14.2. Office crossword puzzle.

CHAPTER 15

Arthur's Computer Disaster

Marc Brown

New York: Scholastic, 1997

Summary

Mother asked Arthur and his friend Buster to leave the computer alone while she was out. But the boys could not resist another chance to play Deep, Dark Sea. When the keyboard crashed to the floor, the panic-stricken pair attempted to solve their problem. However, Mom was able to rectify the situation.

Theme

Specific expertise is needed to appropriately use technology in the workplace. The computer also provides many opportunities for individuals to earn a living at home.

Content Related Concepts

computer technology, tax season

Content Related Words

computer, computer manual, computer games

Activities

1. Arthur has his own homepage. Contact him at http://pbs.bilkent.edu.tr/wgbh/pages/arthur/.

2. Arthur and his mother used the same computer, but for different reasons. Mother's use was work-related. Arthur played computer games. Have the children make up a list of different reasons for using a computer. Put these in categories such as computer games, instructional activities, home management, and so forth.

3. Under the category of computer games, make a list of specific games that the children play and indicate if they are educational. What are the most popular games?

4. On a map of the school, indicate how many computers there are in each room. Where are the most computers? Where are the fewest? What purpose do these machines serve? Does the school staff feel they need more computers? Ask the principal or technology teacher how much one computer costs. What items does this include?

5. Analyze a sales slip from the Bits and Bytes store (Figure 15.1). How much will one complete computer setup cost? What items will it include?

Bits and Bytes
1875 Genesee Street
Rochester, New York
14620
(716) 866-4391

Quantity	Number	Description	Unit Price	Total Price
1	AJE078	Computer package	$1,000	$1,000
		Includes monitor, keyboard, CPU, mouse		
1	409H	Scanner	$ 200	$ 200
1	M080	Modem	$ 100	$ 100
1	785D	Mouse pad	$ 29	$ 29
1	415H	Word Processor/spread sheet	$ 150	$ 150
1	998	Electronic atlas	$ 25	$ 25
1	567	Income tax program	$ 30	$ 30

Sold by _____   Subtotal

Date_____   6% Sales Tax

                                        Total price

Sales tax exempt if purchased September 2 –9

5% savings during remodeling sale—September 2-16

Serving our customers since 1980

Fax (716)-872-4469
Bitsandbytes@aol.com

Figure 15.1. Computer sales slip.

6. How much money can the school spend on computers each year? How is it decided which computers will be purchased? How will they be used?

7. If there are computers in the classroom, rules for their use are necessary. Have the children work together to make a set of rules and schedules so that every child has an equal chance to use the computers.

8. Schedule each student for writing time on the computer. This can be a follow-up to classroom lessons or from a list of possible topics (e.g., I would like to meet (name) because. . . ; I would like to go to Disney World because. . . ; I think I learn a lot from television because. . . ; I would be good at walking my neighbor's dog this summer because. . .).

9. Why does Arthur's mother need to have the computer available to her when she is at home? Is this part of her job? Can students guess what she does for a living?

10. Many people now work at home instead of going in to the office or other place of business. Why? What are the advantages and disadvantages of being able to work from one's home? How would it affect the family if mom or dad were able to stay home to work?

11. Is there someone nearby who works at home using today's technology as an integral part of the workday? Ask this person to speak to the class about running a business from home.

12. What other machines would be needed to maintain an office at home (e.g., computer, printer, scanner, fax machine, copy machine). How are office machines advertised? What is a reasonable price for each item? Note: Office equipment can also be bought online from sites such as http://www.henryhall.com.

13. Computers are used by workers in many different occupations. They can be found in automotive garages, at sandwich shops, in art studios, in police cars, and so forth. Have the students ask family members and friends if they use computers in their work. Post the occupations of these people on a bulletin board display.

14. Some jobs, such as coal mining, are very hazardous to the health of the worker. Many hours a day of working at a computer can also cause discomfort to the body, for example, the back and the neck. Carpal tunnel syndrome affects the hands and arms. Have the children ask computer users if they suffer from these or other problems. Note: Many stores and catalogue sales companies are selling furniture that is "ergonomically correct" and is designed to prevent body discomfort for the computer user.

15. Provide computer magazines in the classroom or the Library Media Center for the children to read. What new software packages are available? Is there a section of educational software? How are new programs reviewed? How are computers changing?

16. Arrange time for the library media specialist to present a review of the computer books and magazines housed in the Library Media Center. These materials should represent different skill levels among the children.

17. For additional information on computers, here are the Web sites for five major computer companies:

> Dell: http://www.dell.com
>
> Hewlett Packard: http://www.hp.com
>
> Gateway: http://www.gateway.com
>
> Microsoft: http://www.microsoft.com
>
> Toshiba: http://www.toshiba.com

Students may wish to add to the directory other companies they know.

18. One major computer company uses boxes printed to look like cows. Have the children design a box for an imaginary computer company that would be as unique as the ones that have cowhide printed on the cases.

19. Discuss what happens to all the empty boxes after a computer is installed. Is there a cardboard recycling program in the community? Or, is there value in keeping the boxes?

20. There are many Arthur books. Have each child read one of these books and write a brief book review. Indicate why they think Arthur books are so popular. More Arthur adventures are found on the Arthur series on public television.

21. Crossword Puzzle

These are the words for the crossword puzzle (Figure 15.2, page 91).

Keyboard	Click	Monitor	Computer
Online	Internet	Mouse	Manual
Modem	Mouse pad		

References

Cole, Joanna. *The Magic School Bus Gets Programmed: A Book About Computers*. New York: Scholastic, 1999.

ACROSS

3. The TV-like part of the computer

6. Used to input letters and numbers

8. Goes between the mouse and the work surface

9. A handheld device used to position the cursor and execute commands

DOWN

1. To push the mouse button

2. A device that performs mathematical and word processing tasks

4. Connected to the Internet

5. An international network of computers

7. An instruction booklet and guide

8. Converts data into sound for long distance transmission

Figure 15.2. Computer crossword puzzle.

CHAPTER 16

Pancakes, Pancakes

Eric Carle
New York: Aladdin, 1998

Summary

Jack woke up thinking of pancakes for breakfast. But his mother told him that he would first have to harvest the grain and have it milled into flour. Then he must get eggs and milk, and churn some butter. After building the fire to cook the pancakes and getting some jam from the storage room, Jack helped his mother to mix the batter and cook the pancakes. Finally, it was time for breakfast!

Theme

The work of many hands is required to produce a product.

Content Related Concepts

non-industrial society, agricultural society, flour-making process, food preparation

Content Related Words

mill, sickle, flail, grain, threshing, millstone, griddle

Activities

1. The Middle Ages in Western Europe lasted from approximately AD 500 until around AD 1200. For more background information on this time period, consult a children's encyclopedia, the Internet, or history books in the Library Media Center. Note: The keywords "Middle Ages" will access many web sites on topics such as the manor, the lords and serfs, farming, holidays, and so forth.

2. Many topics on the Middle Ages will be of interest to the students (e.g., castles, tournaments, fairs, knights in armor, lords of the manor, the life of the peasants, the nobility and the artisans, as well as music, art, clothing, and transportation). In groups, have the children research a favorite topic. Note: Arrange to have books on these subjects brought from the Library Media Center to the classroom during this time or put them on reserve for the class.

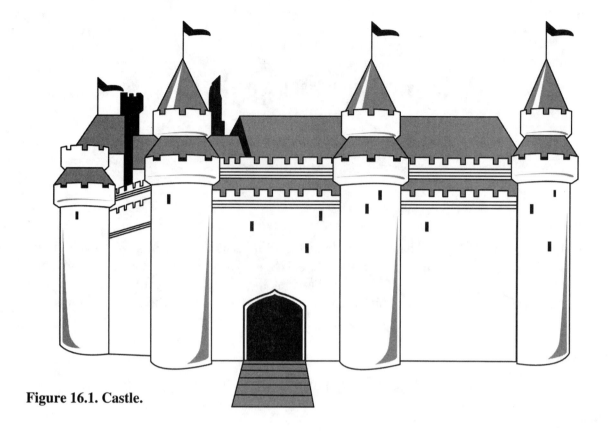

Figure 16.1. Castle.

3. To help students learn about life in the Middle Ages, introduce them to David Macaulay's books (e.g., *Cathedral* and *Castle*). Note: Calendars showing castles are very popular and can also assist the children's research.

4. Discuss how life would be different during the Middle Ages. In fact, practically nothing would be the same as today. At that time, there was no electricity or indoor plumbing, no television, movies, or CD players, no cars, no schools, no postal system, and so on. Also, compare modern and medieval conveniences (e.g., the use of the alarm clock compared with the use of a rooster to wake people up, ox carts versus pickup trucks).

5. The people of the Middle Ages did not have the technology we have now to perform complicated tasks. Divide the class and assign problem-solving topics to each group. Share the results of their brainstorming. Topics might include splitting wood, keeping food items cold, building a bridge, taking a load of produce to market, moving a large statue to the church, cooking over an open fire, and so on.

6. After several readings of the book, ask the children to sequence on storyboards the steps Jack went through to get to enjoy the pancakes (e.g., threshing the wheat, going to the miller, building a fire in the stove). See Figure 16.2.

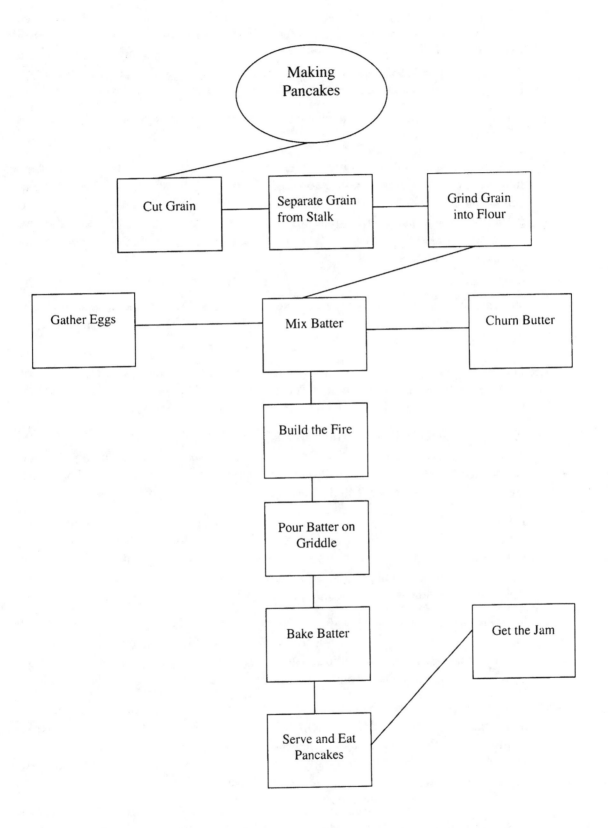

Figure 16.2. Pancake flow chart.

7. Compare the process that Jack followed to the making of pancakes today. Do children understand the difference between making pancakes from scratch and making then from mixes today? How many kinds of pancakes do we have today (e.g., those with blueberries, apples, peaches; those with different syrups, such as maple or blueberry; those made from buckwheat or whole wheat flour). What are the class favorites?

8. For more information about wheat and flour, use the keywords "wheat processing" on the Internet.

9. This story illustrates the steps in a process. Have the children write out their own steps in a process (e.g., getting dressed for school, changing the sheets on a bed, going to school on the school bus, accessing the Internet, packing a lunch, playing a video game, sending e-mail, gift wrapping a package, making macaroni and cheese). Children can also think of school-related processes like long division, memorizing spelling words, and so on.

10. To see the steps of a process at work, arrange a class trip to a pizza or donut shop. What steps are involved? Can any of the steps be interchanged? What happens if a step is left out? Be sure there will be time for a sample. Note: Parental permission should be secured for each child making the trip.

11. Do children know where food comes from before it reaches the store? Make a list of favorite foods and ask, "Where do we get hamburgers?" "How does the milk get from the cow to the buyer?" Have the children think of other scenarios.

12. When pancake batter is cooked on a griddle, several chemical changes occur. The outside of the pancakes oxidizes to become brown and crispy. Bubbles of carbon dioxide are given off as the inside cooks. What is the difference between the cooked pancakes and the ingredients from which they are made?

13. If it is possible, have the children visit a restaurant that serves pancakes, or make pancakes in the classroom. Silver-dollar sized pancakes would work fine. Various toppings such as fruit, chocolate chips, and whipped cream can make this a creative adventure. Note: Parental permission should be secured for each child making the trip. Ask parents to indicate any food allergies or special diets.

14. What do the children normally eat for breakfast? Are weekdays different from weekends? Do children ever go to a restaurant for breakfast? Are there students who generally "skip" breakfast? Have each child illustrate or write a short, informational paragraph on what they eat for breakfast and compare this to what other children in the class eat.

15. In a pre-industrial society, there was much more physical activity exerted to complete a task than today when machines help do the work. Talk about the concept of work. Think of today's machines as "human energy savers." Is it considered "work" to shovel the snow? Decorate for a party? Help a friend move? Run a 5K race? Babysit for a young child? Is a machine always available to help save "energy"?

16. People have generally settled in places where there is running water, that is, a river to provide transportation. After reading this book, can the students tell other reasons for building a community near a source of water? (See Figure 16.3.)

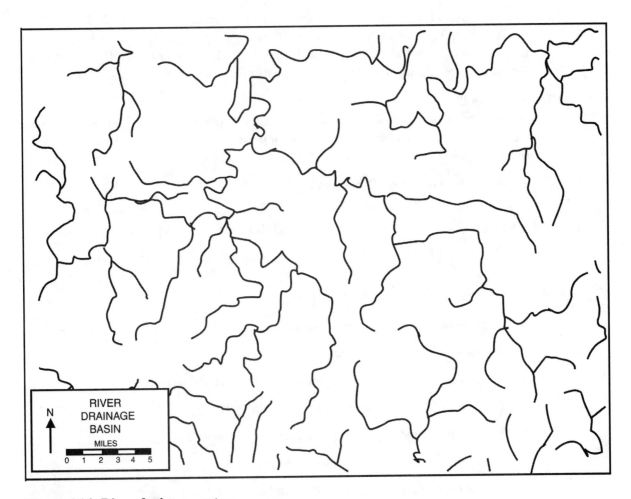

Figure 16.3. River drainage system.

17. In the story, Jack gets some strawberry jam from the cool cellar. How were people in the Middle Ages able to preserve food? Ask someone who enjoys cooking to explain this process to the class. An easy, but perishable, jam that can be made in the classroom is strawberry freezer jam. These are the instructions:

Thaw 2 10-ounce cartons of strawberries

Mash them

Add 3½ cups sugar

Stir until well mixed and sugar is dissolved

Let stand for 20 minutes, stirring occasionally

Add 1 packet of pectin and stir well

Pour into clean canning jars or freezer containers

Refrigerate for 24 hours

Use jam immediately with pancakes, bread, or crackers or freeze until needed

Note: This jam will be thinner than commercial jams and jellies.

18. Borrow several Eric Carle books from the Library Media Center. Mr. Carle's method of illustrating is based on the use of small pieces of colored paper pieced together to make a scene. Have the children study these illustrations and make collages using this method. Note: Old wallpaper books can be of great use for this process.

19. What Am I?
Imagine that people and objects in the story can all communicate with the reader. From their descriptions of themselves, guess who or what they are. Or have children assume the role of an object and tell the class what they do. The class can then guess who they are.

These are the words for "What Am I?"

a. Mill	d. Batter	g. Miller	i. Wheat
b. Pancake	e. Churn	h. Millstone	j. Straw and chaff
c. Flour	f. Flail		

These are the clues to help solve "What Am I?"

1. I am the place where the wheat is made into flour. _____

2. I am a wooden device used for making butter. _____

3. I am an instrument used for separating the grain from the chaff. _____

4. I am an uncooked mixture of flour, eggs, and milk. _____

5. I am turned by moving water and can crush grain into flour. _____

6. I am a grass-like plant, which is the source of grain. _____

7. I am used to make bread, cakes, pies, and cookies. _____

8. I am left behind after the threshing process. _____

9. I supervise the running of the mill. _____

10. I am breakfast bread served with syrup or jam. _____

References

Carle, Eric. *The Grouchy Ladybug*. New York: Thomas Crowell, 1977.

——— . *The Tiny Seed*. London: Hodder and Stoughton, 1987.

Gravett, Christopher. *Castle*. London: Dorling Kindersley, 1994. (An Eyewitness Book)

Langley, Andrew. *Medieval Life*. London: Dorling Kindersley, 2000. (An Eyewitness Book)

Macaulay, David. *Castle*. Boston: Houghton Mifflin, 1977.

——— . *Cathedral*. Boston: Houghton Mifflin, 1973.

CHAPTER 17

Granddaddy's Street Songs

Monalisa DeGross

New York: Hyperion Books for Children, 1999

Summary

Granddaddy used to ride through the streets of Baltimore singing his special songs as he sold his fruits and vegetables. Young Roddy had heard this story from his Granddaddy until he knew it by heart. Still he asked to hear it again and again.

Theme

Appropriate care of products and competitive marketing strategies help to create a successful livelihood for this salesman.

Content Related Concepts

salesmanship, marketing, Camden Market, street vendors

Content Related Words

"arabbin," toe-heel, mahogany, stall, Thermos, gimmick, produce, cobblestone

Activities

1. Baltimore is a large city in the United States. Locate it on the map of Maryland (see Figure 17.1, page 100). Indicate the states and bodies of water that border it. Note: For an outline map of the United States see *Potato: A Tale of the Great Depression* (Chapter 2).

2. Learn some facts about Baltimore using information from the Internet or from travel books. Students probably know that there are many sports teams in Baltimore, but do they know about Francis Scott Key and Fort McHenry or the Inner Harbor, the Maryland Science Center, and the National Aquarium? The keywords "Baltimore, Maryland" will access these topics as well as restaurants, lodging, transportation, events, and weather.

3. Have the children talk to people who were teenagers or adults in 1955. What can these people tell the youngsters about that time—history, sports, music, movies, and so forth? Do any of them have items from that time (e.g., high school yearbooks, old magazines, family photos)?

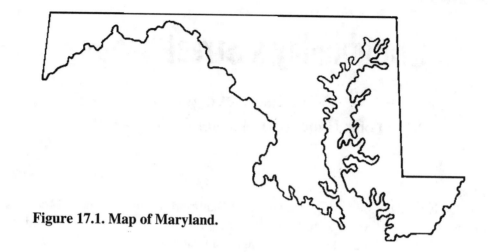

Figure 17.1. Map of Maryland.

4. Music from 1955 may be appealing to the students. Play some selections by performers such as Elvis Presley. How would these be different from the songs Granddaddy sang?

5. Ask the library media specialist to identify events that occurred in 1955. How have these affected the lives of the students today? How is life different today? Note: Yearbooks and encyclopedias are good sources of photos and information.

6. Granddaddy was very successful selling his fruits and vegetables. Why? Working in small groups, have the children write out "Granddaddy's Rules of Salesmanship." Compare the different lists. Should salesmen today follow rules like these? Have the children role play the selling of items to one another (e.g., school sweatshirts, subscriptions to a computer magazine, boxes of candy).

7. What items was Granddaddy selling? What did he need to help him get around town? What gimmicks did he use to get people to buy his goods? Do vendors still deliver goods to customers at home? Is there an outdoor farm market where the children live? How do we buy fruits and vegetables today? Discuss these.

8. Have the children design a sign that Granddaddy could have put on the side of his wagon to advertise his business.

9. Granddaddy did a good job to make money for his family. But he also did a good job because he was proud of his work. What rewards do students earn for doing a good job? Should students be paid or get prizes for receiving good grades? What do they think?

10. Granddaddy kept his fruits and vegetables in the shade. What will the direct sun do to fruit that is left out? Put two or three pieces of fruit in the sun for several days. Compare them to similar food that has been kept in the shade or in a refrigerator. Where is the best place to store fruit to keep it fresh?

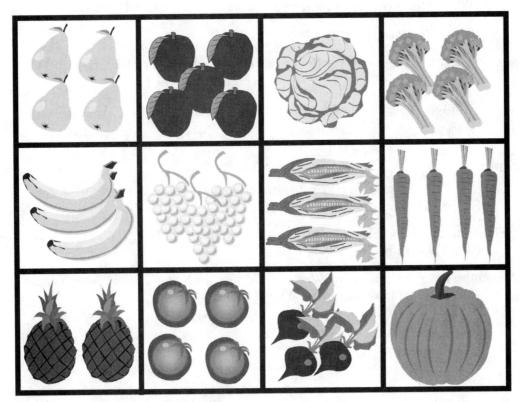

Figure 17.2. Fruits and vegetables.

11. Granddaddy went to Camden Market to pick up the food he later sold. Today a visitor to downtown Baltimore could visit the Lexington Market to buy fresh products. Learn more about this Market on the Internet at http://www.lexingtonmarket.com. What goods are sold there? What special Baltimore foods can be found?

12. Granddaddy was clever and made up songs about the fruits and vegetables he sold. Have the children pick a fruit or vegetable and compose a song or chant to sell their product.

13. Today food is advertised in newspaper flyers. How do these flyers attract the shopper's attention? What do the customers want to know about the products? List the different fruits and vegetables shown in the grocery ads of the newspaper. Figure out the cost per pound for each selection. Which are the most expensive? Which are the least expensive? Are all items sold by the pound? Compare prices from different stores.

14. Granddaddy was always accompanied by his horse, his wagon, and his Thermos bottle filled with iced coffee. What is a Thermos bottle? How does it keep liquids both hot and cold? Try this experiment. Fill one Thermos bottle with either hot or cold liquid and seal it. Fill a noninsulated container with a similar hot or cold liquid, cover it and let it stand at room temperature. Measure the temperature of both hot/cold liquids after two or three hours. Ask the children to explain what happened. Note: Large "coffee

butlers" or Thermos carafes with pumps on them are used in many coffee shops today. What is the advantage of these containers? Are there disadvantages?

15. Crossword Puzzle

These are the words for the crossword puzzle (Figure 17.3, page 103).

Onion	Corn	Pepper	Tomato
Lettuce	Peach	Potato	Celery
Honeydew	Cantaloupe	Strawberry	Cherries

References

Ehlert, Lois. *Eating the Alphabet: Fruits and Vegetables from A to Z.* New York: Econo-Clad Books, 1999.

Harrison, James, and Eleanor Van Zandt. *The Young People's Atlas of the United States.* New York: Kingfisher, 1992.

Jennings, Peter, and Todd Brewster. *The Century for Young People.* New York: Random House (A Doubleday Book for Young Readers), 1999.

ACROSS

1. This vegetable grows in stalks

2. A green melon

4. One of the season's first berries, its seeds are on the outside

6. This round red object is a fruit with its seeds inside

10. These small red fruits have pits inside

11. This brown or red vegetable must be dug up to be used

DOWN

1. The inside of this melon is orange when it is ripe

3. There are many varieties of this leafy vegetable

5. Green, bell-shaped, or pointed. Some are very hot

7. It can make you cry

8. Similar in size to an apple. This fruit has a large pit inside

9. Native Americans called this maize

Figure 17.3. Fruits and vegetables crossword puzzle.

CHAPTER 18

Workshop

Andrew Clements
New York: Clarion Books, 1999

Summary

The definition of each tool in the workshop is explained in narrative form with an illustration. The book also portrays the thrill and pride that the men have in their workmanship as they create the carousel.

Theme

Producing an artistic piece requires the use of many skills and tools.

Content Related Concepts

hand tools, manual labor, power tools

Content Related Words

ruler, ax, saw, hammer, anvil, grinder, chisel, shears, knife, screwdriver, drill, pliers, wrench, toolbox, profit

Activities

1. *Workshop* contains a listing of tools used for woodworking. There are many tools that are used together to achieve a desired purpose. Have children select one of the following topics and find out what tools would be needed to perform this task. They should give an explanation of each step and include an illustration. Fasten these together to make a class booklet. Here is the list of activities:

Baking and frosting a cake	Painting a picture
Fixing a bicycle tire	Making an ice cream sundae
Polishing shoes	Mopping the floor
Painting a table	Slicing and serving a pizza
Making doll clothes	Putting pictures in a scrapbook
Knitting a sweater	Sewing on a button
Making a sandwich	

Note: Children can work alone or in small groups.

2. The illustrations in *Workshop* show the beauty of the various wood grains. Obtain some samples of different wood grains from a lumberyard or bring in small pieces of furniture to show the grain. Companies that sell varnish and other wood finishing materials often publish pamphlets showing their line of finishes as they cover different wood grains. Bring some in. What is the difference between hard woods like oak and soft woods like pine? Why are certain woods like ash used for specific purposes, for example, baseball bats?

3. What items are still made from wood today? What materials are replacing real wood, for example, plastics? Have each child select five items of furniture in his or her home. Are these made from wood? Are parts of an item made of nonwood? Are some of the items made entirely of nonwood materials? Compare lists.

4. The instruments illustrated in the book each show a use of the six simple machines or a combination of them. The simple machines are the wheel and axle, the pulley, the wedge, the lever, the inclined plane, and the screw. How do these tools help the woodcrafter? Have the teacher find other simple machine instruments in the kitchen utensil drawer and demonstrate their use of the six simple machines to the children. What simple machines are used by each utensil? A knife is a wedge; a corkscrew is a screw; a rolling pin is a wheel and axle; a bottle opener is a lever; a pancake turner is a wedge; a doorstop is an inclined plane.

5. Can the children think of complex machines that are a combination of simple machines (e.g., a bulldozer, exercise equipment, a bicycle)? Have the children create their own new work-saving devices using the six simple machines.

6. Make a display of old hand tools. These may be found at a garage sale, an auction, from a grandfather, and so forth. Remember that some of these tools may be of great value monetarily or as sentimental pieces. An active demonstration by the teacher or volunteer would be best for introducing the tools. Note: Children should be cautioned not to handle the tools as they may contain sharp edges. Tools should not be left lying unattended.

MASTERCRAFT

Finest quality hand tools for your collection

Hammers	$14.98 to $24.98
Chisels	$7.98 to $10.98
Planes	$24.98 to $35.98
Screwdrivers	$10.98 to $15.98
Pliers	$14.98 to $19.98

See our complete collection of saws, wrenches,

toolboxes and wood finishes

Murray's Hardware Store
701 State Street
(609) 344-7799

Figure 18.1. Tool sale advertisement.

7. The following exercise about hand tools can help the children learn more about these common implements. Have the children pantomime the action of using the tool as they match the words to the definition.

    a. Hammer   1. a tool used to exert a force against an object

    b. Chisel   2. a metal cutting and shaping tool made with a beveled edge

    c. Screwdriver 3. a cutting tool with a thin metal blade

    d. Plane   4. a tool used for gripping, bending, and holding

    e. Saw   5. a tool for smoothing and leveling

    f. Pliers   6. a tool used to fasten, tighten, adjust, or attach by means of a screw

8. Ask a volunteer or a sales associate in a hardware store to visit your class and explain the difference between hand tools and power tools. Could they demonstrate these for the children? Further information can be found in newspaper flyers from hardware and

equipment stores. These descriptions should include information on the tool's construction, its horsepower, uses, guarantee, and so on.

9. Make a chart to compare the advantages and disadvantages of machine-made items and handmade items? Consider the time involved in production, the quality of the workmanship, cost, durability, aesthetic qualities, and so forth.

10. If the school has a display case, ask parents or teachers to bring in hand-crafted items to be put in it. They might include such items as a wooden cuckoo clock from Germany, a carved pelican from Mexico, a woven blanket from Arizona, or a miniature water buffalo statue from Kenya.

11. Handmade items such as the carousel horse, a musical instrument, a sweater, or a quilt can be very expensive. For example, a machine-made quilt may cost $125 while a handmade one would be $600. A machine-made sweater can sell for $30 but a hand-knit one is $150. What is the difference in the way these items are made? Why is there such a price difference? Why would some people be willing to pay the higher price?

12. Have the children discuss the concept of "profit." People cannot maintain a business if they do not make a profit. How does the craftsman decide on a price for the articles he or she has made? How does someone determine how much his or her time and effort is worth? If the children wish to start a business, such as selling lemonade or cookies, mowing lawns or babysitting, what must they charge to make a profit?

13. Have the children select a handmade craft project to do. Use magazines or books from the Library Media Center for ideas or engage the assistance of the art teacher. These publications are particularly bountiful for the holiday season. Note: Patterns for craft items in magazines are often printed in very small scale and must be enlarged according to the directions in the magazine. Use graph paper with larger squares to make the transfer.

14. Information about handcrafted items can be gotten from woodworking societies, such as: http://www.woodking.com/tools/saw.htm or http://woodworking.miningco.com/. Organizations include American Woodworkers Association and The American Association of Woodturners. Search for other topics such as quilting, building miniatures, and similar crafts.

15. Word Search

   These are the words in the word search (Figure 18.2, page 109).

Ruler	Anvil	Shears	Hammer
Ax	Grinder	Knife	Pliers
Saw	Chisel	Screwdriver	

References

Bramlett, Tim. *A Kid's Guide to Crafts: Wood Projects*. Mechanicsburg, PA: Stackpole Books, 1997.

```
F R U B Z T R S T B T H K O C X R D K E
Y U B Z E E U V A Z Y A F Q A V O Z Y P
G O V S I I L H M L C M T D H I G T X L
A R E U U X E K K C I M L R Y Y F C T I
W D X A I D R P S F O E K E E R Q L I E
N G D Q O D A L H G G R H D R C J N V R
P T R R I E R C V L N C J N E Q U Z A S
M B I Y J O Q X C L E L B I V E Y T L U
Q F D L W J L S T Z I U G R I V E S Y L
V Z L B A R U A Z I R U S G R S U H C Y
Y A C F N W C H I S E L V C D Z N E U Z
C C X M V U O G R I K D L J W U X A D X
W W Y M I D H S N K B R L Q E Q C R M M
G M X B L W O L J S A K X V R T L S B A
G O K J X E Z V V X X R P V C Y O N T B
L W O K N H D B C W J P G I S X E T D T
K V F Q R A K R X I H M Y Z R M Q L V X
G Y Y I S X G B U D K S A W S O H P M M
M L M J V K Y H A D E M H B O D E B H E
B V P T O T J V X Y E F I N K E C V K V
```

1. Used to measure __ __ __ __ __
2. Used to make indentations in wood or stone __ __ __ __ __ __
3. Used to pound nails __ __ __ __ __ __
4. Used to hold objects __ __ __ __ __ __ __
5. A solid mass of steel which is pounded upon __ __ __ __ __
6. A rotating stone used to sharpen or shape metal __ __ __ __ __ __ __

7. Used to chop or split wood __ __
8. Large scissors __ __ __ __ __ __
9. A tooth-edged object used for cutting __ __ __
10. A wedge-like blade used for carving __ __ __ __ __
11. Used to tighten screws

    __ __ __ __ __ __ __ __ __ __ __

Figure 18.2. Tool word search.

CHAPTER 19

Night Shift Daddy

Eileen Spinelli

New York: Hyperion Books for Children, 2000

Summary

A little girl and her father share a warm, loving relationship built around Daddy's night-shift job.

Theme

Different jobs demand varied work hours.

Content Related Concepts

Shift work, night shift, on call

Content Related Words

Thermal, bundled up, punctual, consistent

Activities

1. Make a list of jobs that are carried out at night. These may be put into two classifications, those in which there is interaction between the worker and a customer and those that are performed "behind the scenes." Discuss the following examples of jobs:

donut shop waitress	maintenance crew worker
discount department store clerk	repair worker
service station attendant	road worker
police officer	security guard
fire fighter	store designer
hospital worker	baker
convenience store clerk	food preparer
bus station manager	grocery store staff
airport worker	factory employee

weather forecaster	telephone operator
truck driver	street sweeper
911 dispatcher	caregiver or babysitter
cleaning staff	radio disc jockey

2. In the story, why does Daddy work at night? Why can't this job be done during the day?

3. Are there children of night-shift dads or moms in the classroom? Ask them to tell how their family adapts to Dad's or Mom's schedule.

4. There are usually three shifts in a day although the times they encompass may vary from one job to another. In some types of jobs, the "morning" shift is from 5 AM to 1 PM. The "swing" shift is from 1 PM to 9 PM. The late or "graveyard" shift is from 9 PM to 5 AM. Work times may be different from job to job or from week to week. How long does the worker stay with one shift before changing, or is this a permanent assignment? How does the family adapt when there is a constant change? How do workers maintain productivity when their schedules shift and sleep hours may be disrupted? If there is a big change in the school day, how are the students affected?

5. Some parents may have a job in which they are "on call." This means they may have to go in to work at unscheduled times, for example, physicians. How do they find out when they must go to work? Will they be doing their regular duties during this time? Will they know how long they will be there? What other jobs may involve being "on call?"

6. Daddy took the bus to work in the story. How do the children's dads and moms get to work (e.g., car, bus, subway, train, walking). Make a survey of how parents travel to work and graph the results. How do students get to school?

7. Some people tend to be "morning persons"—that is, they do their best work early in the day. Others do better at night. If the children had a choice of being "morning persons" or "night persons," which would they choose? What reasons do they give? How does this relate to working at a job?

8. Ask someone who works at night to share his or her experiences with the class. What are the advantages of working the night shift? What are the disadvantages? Do they rely on anything to help fill in the hours, for example, the radio? Note: The scheduling of the speaker must be flexible and work around the speaker's work hours. Or this could be a tape-recorded interview.

9. A good worker is punctual and consistent. *Punctual* means that they are on time. *Consistent* means that they always act in the same manner with the same care for their work. Are there other qualities that characterize a good worker? How can students be good workers? Are punctuality and consistency enough? Who judges whether a child is a good student? What are the rewards for being a good student?

10. Anyone can be a good student. Select a positive quality for each student and make an award certificate to announce this to the class. Students may wish to attach pictures of themselves to the certificates and post these on the wall. Students may be "the best," for award certificate purposes, for academic and nonacademic reasons (e.g., they take good care of the plants or animals, they tally the lunch count and take it to the office, they play an instrument for the class, they bring in the weather forecast).

11. The little girl in the story needed to know when it was time for Daddy to go to work and when it was time for him to come home. Practice telling time using manila folders that show the clock face inside and have movable hands made of construction paper that are attached to the folder with a brass fastener (Figures 19.1, 19.2). The teacher and students can take turns calling out times to be positioned on the folder. Or select a specific time and have the children place it on their clock.

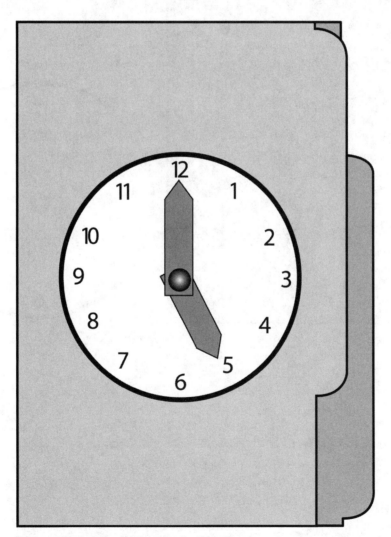

Figure 19.1. File folder clock diagram.

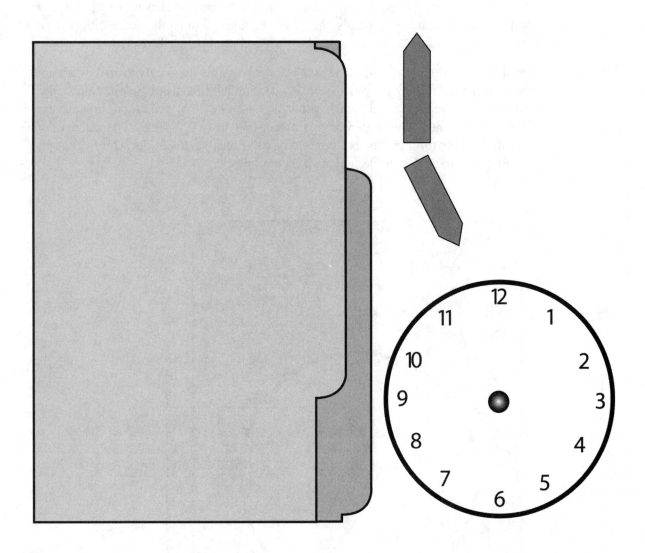

Figure 19.2. File folder clock pattern.

12. Identify important times throughout the day (e.g., reading class, lunch, recess, gym class, sharing time). Have the children practice putting the times of these events onto their clock faces.

13. The little girl and her father loved to read together. This is very important and helps children to become better readers. Make a list of reasons why parents or other older persons should read to children.

14. What older person reads to the class (e.g., the classroom teacher, the librarian, a lady on television)? Why do children like to have someone read to them? How does it help with their schoolwork? Can the children read to younger children or older adults?

15. If someone is going to read to the children, what kind of book would children want (e.g., adventure stories, stories about families, funny stories, mysteries). Make a list for children to vote for their favorite genres. Ask other classes to do the same survey. Graph the results and compare them.

16. Is there "Sustained Silent Reading" time in the school? If not, would it be possible to set aside some time each day when everyone in the school reads? What are some other ways to encourage children to read?

17. Math Puzzle
    Find the letter that corresponds to each number. Use these numbers to fill in the blanks. This will be a line from the book.

A	B	C	D	E	F	G	H	I	J	K	L	M
1	2	3	4	5	6	7	8	9	10	11	12	13

N	O	P	Q	R	S	T	U	V	W	X	Y	Z
14	15	16	17	18	19	20	21	22	23	24	25	26

```
8   15  23      3   15  26  25      1   18  5
__  __  __      __  __  __  __      __  __  __

20  8   15  19  5       20  15  5   19
__  __  __  __  __      __  __  __  __
```

Note: Further instructions for math puzzles are found in Chapter 6, *Waiting for the Evening Star*.

References

Spinelli, Eileen. *When Mama Comes Home Tonight*. New York: Simon & Schuster, 1998.

PART III

WORK COMMUNITIES

CHAPTER 20

The Village of Round and Square Houses

Ann Grifalconi

Boston: Little, Brown, 1986

Summary

Village life was happy and peaceful for the boys and girls of Tos. After dinner the men smoked and talked of farming. Grandma would tell the story of the night long ago when Naka thundered out her fury. When the volcanic eruption was over, all of the people were covered with gray ash. Everyone had survived, along with two huts in the village—one round and one square.

Theme

In a highly functional community, everyone has an important job to do.

Content Related Concepts

volcanic eruption, division of labor, agricultural society, ancestor spirits

Content Related Words

cassava root, *fou fou*, lava, ash, multiculturalism

Activities

1. The setting is very important to the understanding of this book. Describe the setting. Does the book take place in a big city or a rural area? Is this an industrial society or an agricultural one? How do students think the lives of the villagers in the book compare with those people who live in the capital city of Yaounde? Note: There are one million people living in the capital city.

Figure 20.1. Map of Africa.

119

Figure 20.2. Map of West Africa.

2. Cameroon is in Africa on the Atlantic Ocean. What neighboring countries border it? Where is the equator in reference to this country? How does this compare with where the United States is? What climate would one expect to find on the equator? Note: Remember that as the elevation of the land increases, the temperature drops. It is possible to be situated on the equator and still be relatively cool.

3. The rainfall in Cameroon greatly influences the way people live. There are three regions of the country—one near Mount Cameroon on the coast where there is nearly 400 inches of rain a year, one which is a temperate central area with 60–80 inches of rain a year, and finally, one in which the interior of the country is very dry and has only about 12 inches of rain each year. Compare these figures to rainfall statistics for the community where the students live. How does rainfall affect temperature, vegetation, occupations, recreation, type of housing, and so on?

4. The following chart gives the average high and low temperatures and days of rainfall for each month of the year in Cameroon. What are the hottest months? What are the coldest? Which are the rainiest? Which are the driest? How does this compare to where the children live? What can children learn from the chart? Are there places in the United States with temperatures like those in Cameroon? Are there areas of rainfall comparable to the figures in Activity 3? Have the children graph these figures. If possible, graph figures for the local community and compare the two sets of numbers. Note: Statistics on the chart were taken at Yaounde.

Cameroon Temperature and Days of Rainfall

	Jan.	Feb.	Mar.	Apr.	May	June
Hi Temp	84	84	84	84	82	81
Lo Temp	66	66	66	66	66	66
Rain Days	3	5	13	15	18	17
	July	Aug.	Sept.	Oct.	Nov.	Dec.
Hi Temp	81	81	81	81	82	82
Lo Temp	66	64	66	64	66	66
Rain Days	11	10	20	24	14	4

Figure 20.3. Temperature and rainfall chart.

5. To learn more about Cameroon, access the Internet using the name of this country. There will be a variety of Web sites. The teacher may wish to present a series of short topics which would enhance the information presented in *The Village of Round and Square Houses*.

6. Cameroon has two volcanoes that have shown volcanic activity in recent years: Mt. Cameroon (13,435 feet high) in 1982 and Lake Nyos (3,011 feet high) in 1986. Have the children invent their own legends about why the volcano erupts. Note: Review the word "legend" as an introduction to the writing.

7. The ash, which covered the village after the eruption, acts as a natural fertilizer. Why is fertilizer used? Are there different kinds? Do they serve different purposes? Ask a sales associate at a lawn and garden store to list some of the more common fertilizers. What do they contain? What do the numbers like 5-10-5 mean?

8. Illustrations are very important in a storybook. What factual information can the students obtain from looking at the illustrations in the book (e.g., the women wear a scarf over their head and wear earrings, the children help to prepare the meal). Looking at the illustrations can also be used as a pre-reading activity.

9. There are many things to understand about a different culture. By reading this book, what can the children learn about food, utensils, clothing, jewelry, housing, school, entertainment, religious beliefs, education, and so on? Aid the reading of the book with information from the Internet. Note: Teachers may be especially interested in educational practices in Cameroon.

10. Make a list of the different jobs done in this African society, then match the jobs to the people in the book who always did them. How does this division of labor occur in the school or the family when there is a big event taking place? Here are four events to be planned:

    a. An Art and Music Evening for parents at the school. Different musical groups will perform and an example of each student's artwork will be on display. Jobs to be done include write invitations, prepare refreshments, set up stage, arrange artwork, appoint coatroom attendants, set up computer exhibit, coordinate stage and backstage workers, and so on. How will the jobs be assigned?

    b. A clean-up day around the school or other public area. Brainstorm what needs to be done by teachers, administrators, student council members, lower graders, middle graders, upper graders, janitors, cafeteria workers. Will volunteers be asked to join in?

    c. A reunion of the Ambrose family. Jobs include write invitations, find a place for the event, draw directions to get there, arrange food and games, set up tables and utensils, clean up, buy door prizes, arrange overnight accommodations, and so on.

    d. Discuss the tasks that must be done in the classroom. How are helpers chosen? Is this a rotating schedule or does it stay the same? What do the children learn from helping out in the classroom? Is this similar to what the African children do in the story?

11. The study of other cultures is sometimes known as multiculturalism. Discuss what this term means and name some other cultures (e.g., the Amish, the Seminole Indians, the Irish). What different groups are represented in the classroom? Have a diversity day in which students share a piece of their cultural heritage with the others.

12. One of the ways to learn about other cultures is to study their artwork. Discuss objects pictured in an African art book borrowed from the Library Media Center or the community library. Someone in the community who collects African art may be willing to present a talk for the students.

13. The people in the village ate yams and corn, which they grew. They also hunted for rabbit and fished in the stream. Cassava root or fou fou was the main staple in their diet. What is *fou fou*? What part does it play in the diet of these people? Look up "cassava root" on the Internet for additional information. What are the staples of the American diet? Why is the American diet so much more varied?

14. Students may not be familiar with yams. Bring some in. They can be microwaved easily. Cut each yam in half across the middle and pierce the skin in five or six places. Microwave the yam for about 10 minutes. Children should use a microwave oven only under adult supervision. Cool for 10 or 15 minutes. Make a cone from a paper towel and set the potato in the towel. Forks or spoons can be used to eat the contents of the yam from the skin. Add salt and pepper and butter if desired. In a conventional oven, bake the yams 45 minutes to an hour. Note: Small yams are preferable and would take less time to bake. Yams are extremely hot when they are baked and children should be warned to let them cool before they touch or eat them. Be sure to check for food allergies before allowing the students to eat the yams.

15. Everyone in the village had a specific job. This is called the division of labor. What jobs are performed by the men, the women, and the children? Do we divide our jobs like this in our American culture? Are there jobs that are considered to be only for men or only for women? Look at the concept of work in other units in this book, for example, Chapter 4, *Mama Is a Miner*.

16. As a closing activity, have the children choose whether they would rather live in an agricultural village in Africa or in their industrial society in America. Have them write a paragraph explaining why.

17. Crossword Puzzle

    These are the words for the crossword puzzle (Figure 20.4, page 124).

Lava	Yam	Village	Africa
Tobacco	Naka	Tos	Gran'pa Oma
Ashes	Coffee	Volcano	Fou fou

References

Merrill, Yvonne. *Hands-On Africa: Art Activities for All Ages*. Salt Lake City, UT: Kits Publishing, 2000.

Steele, Philip. *The Kingfisher Young People's Atlas of the World*. New York: Kingfisher, 1997.

ACROSS

1. The home of round and square houses
3. The story took place on this continent
4. A small village in the Cameroons
8. Similar to a sweetpotato
9. A tall leafy plant
10. Hot flowing rock
11. Daily food of the villagers

DOWN

2. The leader of the village
3. These covered the people after the eruption
5. The mountain by the village
6. Grows as beans on trees
7. A place where molten rock and ash come out of the ground

Figure 20.4. West Africa crossword puzzle.

CHAPTER 21

Raising Yoder's Barn

Jane Yolen
Boston: Little, Brown, 1998

Summary

A late night fire destroys Yoder's barn, but a few days later the Amish community gathered to raise a new one.

Theme

Teamwork is essential to the well-being of a community.

Content Related Concepts

agrarian society, pre-industrial society, communal working, bucket brigade

Content Related Words

Amish, cooperation, bees, quilts, buggy, sickle, windmill, stall, timbers, cellar hole, foreman

Activities

1. Note: Numerous groups of German farm families migrated to the United States in the early 1700s seeking religious freedom. Collectively they are called Pennsylvania Dutch, after a mispronunciation of the word *Deutsch*, or German. Included as Pennsylvania Dutch are the Mennonites, the Church of the Brethren, the Moravians, and the Amish. The Amish comprise the largest of these groups today and it is their name that will be used exclusively in this unit. When researching information on these people in a reference book or on the Internet, however, one should use both names—Amish and Pennsylvania Dutch.

2. The Amish originally settled in Pennsylvania where founder William Penn had organized a colony that observed religious tolerance. Over the years these people have moved into several other states as well as Canada. Today the largest numbers of Amish are in Pennsylvania, Ohio, Indiana, and Illinois. Smaller settlements include Iowa, Nebraska, Missouri, Kansas, Michigan, and Ontario (Canada). States that have the smallest number of Amish are Maryland, Virginia, North Dakota, Minnesota, Arkansas, Oklahoma, and Mississippi. Mark the states in three different styles to indicate the

125

population density of the three groups of Amish. Note: There is an outline map of the United States in Chapter 2, *Potato: A Tale of the Great Depression*. Ontario, Canada, lies just to the north of New York State across Lake Ontario.

3. *The Folks in the Valley: A Pennsylvania Dutch ABC*, by Jim Aylesworth is an excellent work that should appeal to children and give them much information on the Amish. This book could be read in preparation for *Raising Yoder's Barn*.

4. Teaching and library resources include books such as *A History of the Amish* by Steven Nolt, *The Amish School* by Sara E. Fisher and Rachel K. Stahl, and *Amish Barns and Houses* by Stephen Scott. These are available from Good Books, P.O. Box 419, Intercourse, PA 17534, phone: 1-800-762-7171. An extensive list of other titles is available.

5. A map and visitor's guide to the Amish in the Lancaster, Pennsylvania, area is available from the Pennsylvania Dutch Convention and Visitor's Bureau at 1-800-PA-DUTCH.

6. When the Amish came to America, they settled in rural areas where they could be farmers. Their way of life today is essentially the same as it was in the early 1700s. They use no electricity, no automobiles, no TVs, no tractors, no telephones, no indoor plumbing, or most other modern conveniences. They may ride in autos or trains driven by non-Amish, speak on another's telephone, and in some cases, will allow the use of gas lamps and milking machines. With the children, discuss the difference between the Amish of today and mainstream America. Read the list below and decide which items might be found in an Amish home and which would not.

In an Amish home?	Yes	No
a Bible		
an electric vacuum cleaner		
gas lamps		
musical instruments		
a wood burning stove		
electric curling iron		
computer games		
bicycles		
electric alarm clock		
shovels and rakes		
a wagon		
an iron frying pan		
metal washtubs		
an electric toaster		

7. Have the children select one item that is not normally used by the Amish, for example, electricity. Have them write an essay titled, "My Life Without _____." Students may choose items such as video games, hair dryers, popcorn makers, dishwashers, and so forth. These essays may be shared orally or posted on a bulletin board.

Figure 21.1. Amish buggy traffic sign.

8. Amish families still speak a dialect of the German language at home. English is used for their contact with non-Amish and is not taught until children reach school age. Do the children in today's classroom speak other languages? Are other languages spoken in the home? If so, what languages? Graph the results of the inquiry.

9. The following statements about the Amish schools are all true. Discuss these with the children by comparing them with the children's school.

Amish schools?	Yes	No
Children often start school unable to speak English.		
Amish schools go only to the eighth grade.		
Amish schools reflect Amish values and culture.		
In September parents gather to clean the schoolhouse.		
The Amish still use one-room schoolhouses.		
Classes include scripture reading, history, English, spelling, geography, reading, arithmetic, and health.		
There are special books and magazines published to help Amish teachers to improve their skills.		
Most Amish teachers are young unmarried women.		
Report cards are sent home six times a year.		
Parents help to produce a Christmas program yearly.		
Parents may visit the school with no previous notice.		
There are separate schools for children with special needs.		
Amish education aims to prepare children to be God-fearing, hard-working, and self-supporting.		

10. Amish families take turns hosting a small group of worshippers each Sunday. There is no ordained leader and all members contribute to a simple service based on scripture. A shared meal is served in the afternoon. How does this compare with worship traditions for the children and their family?

11. The Amish can be referred to as a "society apart," yet they are a "people together." This involves the concept of cooperation or communal working. The Amish will band together to help a family in need. Typically, this is the need for a new barn or a new house. The Amish will also work together on farming chores such as harvesting or threshing—jobs that are too difficult for one farmer. In the case of Mr. Yoder, this communal gathering, or barn raising, meant that his family would have a new barn in a day or two. How was it possible for this to happen so quickly? Note: Not just the men were involved in the barn raising. Women and children had very important roles.

12. Have the children discuss what *cooperation* and *communal working* mean. When do the children work communally (e.g., planning a holiday party, conducting a winter coat drive, rehearsing programs for American Education Week, doing a scout project). Other examples of teamwork among adults might include the pit crew at an auto race, a team of lawyers working for one cause, members of a political campaign staff, and so on.

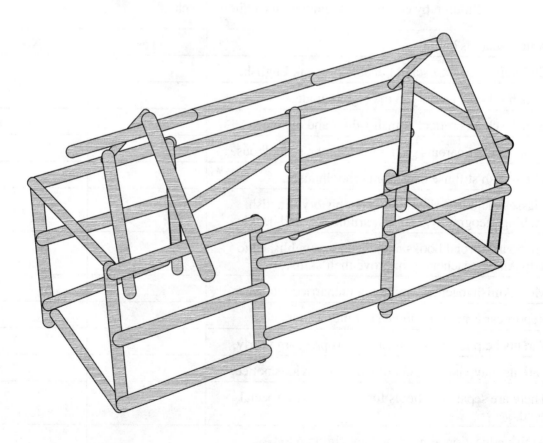

Figure 21.2. Popsicle-stick barn.

13. The Amish do not use smoke alarms in their houses or barns. This lack of warning leads to a longer period of time before help can be summoned if there is fire. This can result in increased damage to buildings and possibly death. Should it be a law to require the use of smoke alarms, not just in Amish homes, but in all homes across America? Have a debate between those for smoke alarm laws and those who prefer the present system.

14. The Amish are especially known for their excellent craftsmanship in making furniture and quilts. Remember that these are all made by hand. Quilts, for example, consist of patched pieces held together with thousands of stitches. The actual quilting of the top cover to a backing piece is done at social gatherings known as "bees." Have the children design paper quilt squares based on a theme for a quilt. Then fasten the squares together or paste them on a backing sheet for a hall display. Note: Squares of white material and permanent magic markers can produce a lasting quilt. In many areas, women of a local church will assemble and quilt the pieces.

15. The Amish wear very plain clothing—dark or black shirts and black trousers for the men and boys. Both wear a flat, black wide-brimmed hat and a black jacket. Men grow beards after they are married. Women and girls wear a black apron over a plain dress, which can be of a dark, nonblack color. Capes are worn to protect against the weather. All women and girls wear a white cap over their pinned up hair. Hooks are used for all fastening instead of buttons, in keeping with their plain, simple ways.

16. Stick figure dolls can be made using wooden paint-stirring sticks for the head and torso. Pipe cleaners or Popsicle sticks can be the arms. Yarn or rafia works fine for hair. Clothing can be made of cloth or dark construction paper. Figures can stand alone if the bottom of the stick is put into a ball of modeling clay. (See Figures 21.3–21.6 on pages 130–33.)

Figure 21.3. Amish boy paint-stick doll diagram.

Figure 21.4. Amish boy paint-stick doll pattern.

Figure 21.5. Amish girl paint-stick doll diagram.

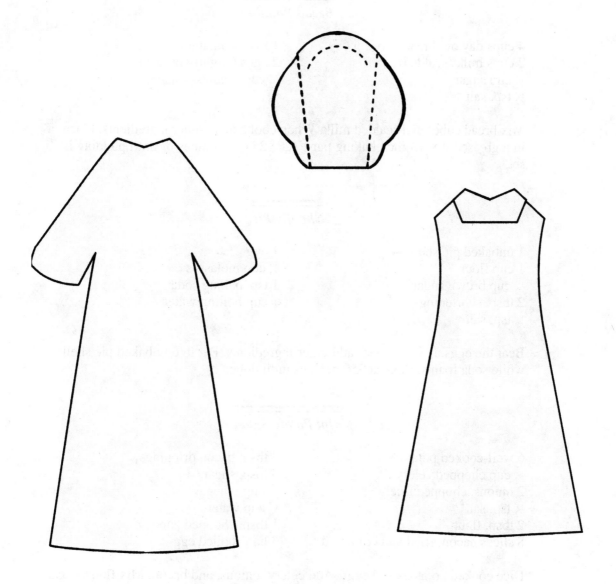

Figure 21.6. Amish girl paint-stick doll pattern.

17. Amish women are well-known for their baked goods. These are often sold to tourists from their front porches. Try these Amish recipes. Note: These items can be made in a carefully supervised classroom. Adults may wish to perform tasks like frying bacon or boiling water. Rules of hygiene should be discussed before beginning work. Also, check any food allergies that the children may have.

Bread Pudding

4 cups day old bread cubes
2 cups milk (scalded)
½ cup sugar
½ tsp. salt

1 tbsp. cinnamon
2 eggs (slightly beaten)
½ cup seedless raisins

Mix bread cubes and scalded milk. When cool add all other ingredients. Place in a greased 9-x-13-inch baking pan. Bake 25–30 minutes or until pudding is set.

Shoofly Pie

1 unbaked pie shell
1 cup flour
½ cup brown sugar
2 tbsp. shortening
½ tsp. salt

1 egg
¾ cup molasses
1 tsp. baking soda
1 cup boiling water

Beat the eggs and molasses; add other ingredients. Put into unbaked pie shell while soda foams. Bake at 350 degrees until done.

Hot Potato Salad

6 well-cooked potatoes
½ cup chopped celery
2 onions, chopped finely
½ tsp. salt
2 tbsp. flour
8 slices bacon, fried and crumbled

4 tbsp. bacon drippings
3 tbsp. sugar
½ cup vinegar
¼ cup water
1 tbsp. chopped parsley
3 hard-boiled eggs

Dice cooked potatoes and eggs. Add celery, onions, and bacon. Mix flour, sugar, vinegar, and water with bacon drippings. Pour over potatoes and mix.

18. Common surnames among the Amish are Stultzfoot, Miller, Lapp, and Yoder. This indicates their German heritage. Other names can indicate different nationalities (e.g., Desjardins is French or French Canadian; Baldacci is Italian; Kocinski is Polish). What names are most common where the children live? Can they tell their nationality by their names? What was the nationally of the settlers in their area?

19. During the unit, children may wish to adopt a common Amish name. Men's names might include Matthew, Samuel, Elam, Christian, Joseph, David, Jacob, Isaac, Elijah, Jonas, Nicholas, Daniel, and Reuben. Women's names might include Betty, Mary Ann, Esther, Rachael, Sarah, Jemima, Ella, Elizabeth, Catherine, Maddie, and Anne.

20. Word Search

    These are the words in the word search (Figure 21.7, page 136).

Cows	Wagon	Shovel	Hoe
Sheep	Plow	Pigs	Hay
Chickens	Harnesses	Horses	Goats
Buggy			

References

Aylesworth, Jim. *The Folks in the Valley: A Pennsylvania Dutch ABC*. New York: Harper Collins, 1992

Fisher, Sara E., and Rachel K. Stahl. *The Amish School*. Intercourse, PA: Good Books, 1986.

Nolt, Steven M. *The History of the Amish*. Intercourse, PA: Good Books, 1992.

Scott, Stephen. *Amish Houses and Barns*. Intercourse, PA: Good Books, (n.d.).

```
T D P I S B K A C V U V S N E K C I H C
P T M G L B S G I P W C D L M C H G M S
X H A Y C T D V D R B A H O P J J N K L
H M E I T E N G H Q J B F B N Z X H O C
N N D I R H U K T O X U E O W G I D E N
R L M B V S E L R S Z G T G L R K V D E
D M Q Z J T S E P D O G Y V Z T L N T D
L P T M B A H V R D E Y Y W R R Q P D N
T O J X O O E O G E M H I H U V Y E Z H
S Z H I F G E H W Q H V X I R Y S Y X M
W N O N N G P S D P V R V V W C W M F J
O Q E I B J K Y J B V F W O O J P G N L
C T R X W W S H P V Z U P L O W K C R K
U I S K G J C F E R I A J S Q V N O R N
N H I F S D N G I Y G D Z Y F S Z L S A
X D K I W A G O N P M J C T G R N Z E J
O H M Z M Y J G S S E S S E N R A H S N
A E C I D L Y A U Q M J Y B W C H S R J
Q K R Q B M N Y W W I E T P R A P R O E
H U V Y N K Y U I C S D O L J W C H H Q
```

1. Large animals that give milk __ __ __ __

2. Their milk is sometimes made into unusual cheese __ __ __ __ __

3. They pull the wagons and buggies __ __ __ __ __ __

4. An enclosed wagon built for carrying people __ __ __ __ __

5. A conveyance used to carry implements and farm goods __ __ __ __ __

6. Animals used as a source of wool __ __ __ __ __

7. Pork products originate with these animals __ __ __ __

8. Domesticated birds used for meat and eggs __ __ __ __ __ __ __ __

9. It is used to break ground before planting crops __ __ __ __ __

10. Dried grass used to feed animals __ __ __

11. A chopping tool used to cultivate gardens __ __ __

12. An implement used for digging __ __ __ __ __ __

13. Straps used to connect the horse to the wagon or plow __ __ __ __ __ __ __ __

Figure 21.7. Amish word search.

CHAPTER 22

The Bobbin Girl

Emily Arnold McCully
New York: Dial Books for Young Readers, 1996

Summary

Rebecca worked in a textile mill in Lowell, Massachusetts. She lived in Mrs. Putney's boardinghouse where she met many girls who were also living away from home and working to save money. But the wages were low and the work was backbreaking. Conditions were unhealthy. No one dared to complain except Judith, who tried to rally the girls to support the formation of a union to work for better conditions. It was the beginning of a long journey for the workers, but one day their needs would be met.

Theme

A safe workplace is important to the well-being of all workers. Management must provide safe, healthy working conditions.

Content Related Concepts

factory, Lowell—City of Spindles, Lyceum lectures, Literary Society, factory slaves, Lowell fever, self reliance

Content Related Words

bobbin, machine, mill, paymaster, overseer, widow, boardinghouse, boarder, dowry, mortgage, academy, relentless, dismissed, traitor

Activities

1. Lowell and Lawrence were important centers of the textile industry. Locate these two cities on the map of Massachusetts (Figure 22.1). Locate the states and the bodies of water that border Massachusetts.

2. Textile mills needed water power to run the machines. What was the nearby source of water in Lowell and Lawrence? Add these rivers to the map. Also locate Massachusetts on a map of the United States. Note: There is an outline map of the United States in Chapter 2 titled *Potato: A Tale of the Great Depression*.

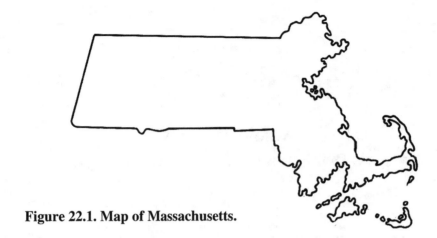

Figure 22.1. Map of Massachusetts.

3. Lowell National Historical Park commemorates the early textile industry in the Lowell-Lawrence area. To get more information about this industry, contact the park at 67 Kirk Street, Lowell, MA 01852-1029, by phone: 508-970-5000, or on the Internet at http://www.nps.gov/lowe/.

4. A demonstration on a portable sewing machine can help students get an idea of the work that went on in the factory, but on a much larger and noisier scale. The illustrations in the book will be helpful explaining this process. Note: The sewing machine not only simulates the noise of the factory that produced textiles. It also shows how a machine can be used to increase productivity.

5. The girls who worked in the mill usually came from the rural areas. They were often alone in the city for the first time. What did they miss about home? How was life different for them now? How did Mrs. Putney try to help? What did the girls do for entertainment in the little free time they had? Have the children compare their lives to that of the girls (e.g., choices for entertainment, amount of personal freedom).

6. When the girls were paid, most of their money went back home to their families. Often the money was used for specific purposes, such as tuition to send a child to school. What other reasons did the girls in the book have for working?

7. Most families today are saving for something special (e.g., a new roof, a car, a trip to Disney World, orthodontic work). Have each child find out something his or her family is saving for and write it on a slip of paper. Collect all of the "wishes" and use them to make a bulletin board. What wishes are most common?

8. This story probably takes place in the 1840s. What was the role of women in society at this time? Did women have the right to go to school? To own things? To vote? Why did the girls work in the mills and not the young boys? Why were the girls guarded so closely in their boardinghouses?

9. The conditions in the mill were appalling. They were noisy, dirty, and unhealthy. Girls worked from 5:30 am until 7:00 pm, with just two short breaks to eat. They were usually fired if they were sick or injured. Many people protested these dreadful conditions.

Have the children pretend they are investigative reporters who wanted to expose these conditions. How might they write this story? Remember that this story is a call to others to help the plight of these girls, but not jeopardize their jobs.

10. The United States was a leading producer of textiles in the nineteenth century. Today the leading textile producers are China, India, Thailand, Korea, Indonesia, and Vietnam. What is responsible for this change? In many areas, workers still toil in "sweat shops." What does this mean? Note: Newspaper articles often cover the topics of sweatshops and illegal immigrants in this country and abroad.

11. A simulation can help students to learn about factory life. Select an item to be mass produced. Choose students to act as workers, overseers, factory owners, customers, boardinghouse proprietors, people looking for employment, and so forth. Have children role-play the various parts, making sure they remember the working conditions that existed in the mid-nineteenth century.

12. Students can simulate a modern "safe" assembly line process, which produces "noodle necklaces." The workforce might include: students to measure the string, cut the string, count the noodles, decorate the noodles, string the necklace, knot the sting, and put each finished necklace into a sandwich bag. Other assembly lines could include making submarine sandwiches, packing books or personal care items for donation to poorer areas, sending a multipage mailing to parents, and so on.

13. Judith made only $1.75 a week as a weaver. This was to be cut by 15 percent. How much money would be cut? How much money would be left? Make up other problems of this type. Check answers with a calculator.

14. In the story, Judith tried to organize the girls to stand up to the employers. Eventually people like her brought about the organization of labor unions, which helped obtain "rights" for the workers. What "rights" did these girls want? What do modern labor unions offer their workers? Are there "rights" that still must be gained? Have any rights been lost?

15. Invite someone from a local factory to speak to the children about modern factories. Topics to be covered would probably include the 40-hour work week, benefits (health insurance, vacations with pay, etc.), safe working conditions in the factory, existence of labor unions, stock ownership, workmen's compensation, and so on. Is there is a labor union in their factory? What do the workers owe to the factory management in return? Note: This is not to imply that all factories provide ideal conditions for working. Many factories and unions are dealing with the problems of downsizing, worker advancement, noise, toxic materials, worker safety, and day care for small children, and so forth.

16. Ralph Waldo Emerson was an important person at this time. He gave hundreds of public lectures each year on topics such as the improvement of society. One lecture was on "self-reliance." After discussing the meaning of this term, have the children write about a time when they had to be self-reliant (e.g., when a parent was ill or away, when they had to watch younger siblings, when they had a project due for school).

17. The book does not have a simple ending that leaves everyone happy. Write a sequel to the story telling what may have happened. Choose Rebecca, Ruth, or Judith as the central character. Keep the character consistent with the personality she had in the story.

18. Compare the author's note at the end of the story to the sequels written by the students. How are they alike or different?

19. Another story about factories in New England is *A River Ran Wild* by Lynne Cherry. This story takes place in nearby New Hampshire and tells the story of how factories changed the way of life in that area.

20. The nineteenth century also saw great advances in the cause of women's rights. Use the Library Media Center or the Internet to learn about women such as Susan B. Anthony. How did their crusade for voting rights parallel the one led by women in the textile cities? What important rights were gained? What working conditions still need to be improved? Note: Access information about Susan B. Anthony from the Web site at http://www.susanbanthonyhouse.org/main.html.

21. Another Web site about the topic of women's rights is the Women's Rights National Historical Park at http://www.nps.gov/wori/ecs.htm/. Information is given about another women's rights advocate, Elizabeth Cady Stanton.

22. *Lyddie* by Katherine Patterson is the story of another girl working in the textile mills. This chapter book could be read as a follow up to *The Bobbin Girl*.

23. Crossword Puzzle

    These are the words for the crossword puzzle (Figure 22.2, page 141).

Yarn	Spindle	Factory	Loom
Bobbin	Wage	Mill	Boardinghouse
Shuttle	Lowell		

References

Cherry, Lynne. *A River Ran Wild*. San Diego: Harcourt Brace Jovanovich, 1992.

Collins, Mary. *The Industrial Revolution*. New York: Children's Press, Grolier Society, 2000.

Harrison, James, and Eleanor Van Zandt. *The Young People's Atlas of the United States*. New York: Kingfisher, 1992.

McCormick, Anita. *The Industrial Revolution in American History*. Berkeley Heights, NJ: Enslow Publishers, 1998.

Patterson, Katherine. *Lyddie*. Hydesville, CA: Lodestar, 1991.

ACROSS

5. Weaving device

6. Young girls rented rooms there

8. Spun from fibers and woven into fabric

10. An industrial city in Massachusetts

DOWN

1. A factory which produced textiles

2. A stick on which fibers are twisted into thread

3. A spool for thread used in weaving

4. A group of buildings where goods were made

7. A device that carries the thread back and forth in weaving

9. Amount of money earned for working

Figure 22.2. *The Bobbin Girl* crossword puzzle.

CHAPTER 23

Worksong

Gary Paulsen

San Diego: Harcourt Brace, 1996

Summary

The work ethic is embodied in the short portraits of these many workers.

Theme

It takes many kinds of workers to keep the community functioning well.

Content Related Concepts

work song, work ethic

Content Related Words

keening, jolting, occupation, nighttime run, errands

Activities

1. The occupations treated in the book are varied. List them on the bulletin board. Are the occupations of the children's parents listed? If not, add these to the job list. Illustrate the board with magazine photos of men and women at work. Note: If there are unemployed parents, ask the kind of work that they hope to get. Stay-at-home moms or dads should be considered as employed for this survey.

2. Additional lists of occupations may be found in the book, *Occupational Outlook Handbook*, compiled by the U.S. Department of Labor. Occupations are classified as industrial, agricultural, business, services, and information. Which of the five categories is most common in the town where the children live, for example, is the town mostly industrial? Is it the center of farm communities? Are many businesses like banks and insurance companies located there? Are there many health services available? Is it a university setting? In five groups, have the children write a one-minute talk answering one of these questions. Include a brief description of their town and the kinds of occupations that are found there. Each group can present their "Hometown Moment" to the others in the class.

3. If possible, obtain a map of the community. On it, place a pin to represent the occupation of each child's parent. Use colored pins so those categories can be seen (e.g., industrial, agricultural, business, service, information). Which are most common? Are there some categories that do not exist in the town? Graph the results.

4. What occupations do the children hope to follow? With the help of the guidance counselor or other adults, organize a career fair. Have displays on various jobs; invite speakers, especially parents, to tell about their jobs; bring in reading materials from the Library Media Center; ask school counselors to talk about the job market; and so forth. Ask each student to make up five questions that they would like answered. After the fair, see how well they did. Note: The *Occupational Outlook Handbook* listed in the reference section of this chapter will provide information on hundreds of career opportunities.

5. Have students create a poster about an occupation that interests them. This can be done on a sheet of poster board using pictures from magazines, sketches, or actual items that are small enough to be attached. Information on the poster should include a definition of the particular job, education or training to be completed, personal requirements needed to enter the field, as well as information about working conditions, benefits, and salary range. These posters make excellent hall displays.

6. Some schools arrange for children to follow someone who has the job that interests the child. This is called "shadowing" and helps the child learn about the demands and rewards of the job. Have each child write a summary of the activities of their day with this role model. Note: Children will need a signed permission slip before participating in the shadowing experience.

7. Children should realize that there is some amount of training necessary for every job. This can range from advanced college degrees to on-the-job experience. Have each child ask two or three people representing different jobs to explain how they learned to do their job. What cost was involved? How long did it take? Must they continue additional training? Can these be put into categories like four-year college, trade school, employer-held training, and so on? Note: Additional information on resume, job shadowing, and future careers are found in Chapter 14, *Mommy's Office*.

8. Have the teacher bring in several examples of newspaper want ads to share with the children or use the ads in Figure 23.1. Do the ads give any information about the employer? Is there a job description? What training or schooling is required? What is the salary? How can one apply? Have the

---

HELP WANTED

Administrative Assistant
Experienced individual with clerical and computer skills. Word, Excel, and Access a must. Full time. Fax resume to 606-873-6241

Route Driver
Class A license required. Full time, benefits. Hours 6 PM to 4 AM, no weekends. Apply in person, 607 Fulton's Run Road, Indiana, PA

Machine Technician
For 3rd Shift-11:00 PM to 7:30 AM Will train, electrical knowledge a plus, start at 8.00 an hour, benefits after 90 days, respond to P.O. Box 752, Rochester, NY 14624

Figure 23.1. Help wanted advertisements.

children imagine that they are in charge of a business that needs employees. Have half the class write an ad that would appeal to qualified candidates. Have the other half write a cover letter for an application for a job they would like. Switch papers and comment. Note: See Activities 18 and 20 in Chapter 14, *Mommy's Office*, for work on resume writing.

9. Do all people work at the same hours of the day? What are normally considered as "daylight hours"? When someone works "at night," what does that mean? What is "shift work"? Which businesses or services are open 24 hours a day? Ask the children when their parents work?

10. Have the children make a chart showing their day. Use this chart as an example.

7:00–8:30	Get up, get ready, eat, find homework
8:30–3:00	Attend school
3:30–5:30	Play; help with supper
5:30–6:30	Cleanup and chores
6:30–8:00	Homework, practice, Scouts, etc.
8:00–9:00	Free

Have the children make a similar chart for mom and dad or other grownup in the house. Do the schedules of the people overlap? When is the busiest time around the house? When is it most quiet? What time is best to ask mom or dad a question? What happens to this schedule on the weekend? How could everyone find more time together?

11. Many occupations expect all employees to wear uniforms. This includes doctors, nurses, fast food servers, service station attendants, and so forth. Many school districts are now considering the possibility of school uniforms for students, and even teachers. What opinions does the class have on this issue? Have the children design a uniform that could be worn at their school. Before beginning, decide if there will be a separate uniform style for boys and girls and one each for summer and winter. (See Figure 23.2.)

12. After becoming familiar with many jobs, have the students write a piece of form poetry about their job. This kind of poetry is explained in Chapter 9, *Blueberries for Sal*. The following is an example of a "five-liner."

> *Teacher*
> *Smart, cheerful*
> *Reading, writing, listening*
> *Caring for her students*
> *Mrs. Smith*

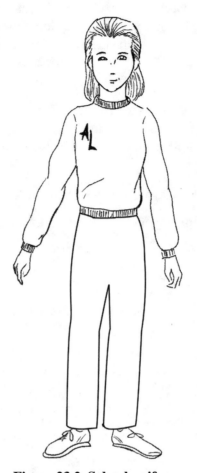

Figure 23.2. School uniform.

13. What is the difference between a salaried employee and one who is paid by the hour? After the students understand the difference, have them answer these questions:

    a. If John works 15 hours at minimum wage ($5.15 per hour), what will he earn?

    b. If Karen works 7 ½ hours at minimum wage, what will she earn?

    c. If Kristen works 25 hours at $8.50 an hour, what will she earn?

    d. Is it better to work 40 hours a week for a whole year for $10.00 an hour or take a salary of $20,000?

    e. Is it better to work 40 hours a week for a whole year for $6.00 an hour or take a salary of $10,000?

    Note: Students may know the concepts involved but may not have practiced with multiple-digit multiplication. In this case the use of a calculator is justified. Or the calculator may be used for checking the answers.

14. Workers need to know about payroll deductions (e.g., taxes, health insurance, retirement, charitable contributions, social security). Use the following pay stub to learn about wages earned and "take home" pay. For example, how many hours does the person work in a week? What is the pay per hour? What is the total amount withheld from this paycheck? What is the take home pay? Have the children make up other examples.

Employee Paycheck Information

Social Security Number	Employee Number	Pay Period Ending
987-65-4321	1079	Sept. 1, 2000
Earning Description	**Current Earnings**	**Year-to-date Earnings**
43.5hours@$11.50	$500.25	$3404.89
Deduction Description	**Current**	**Year-to-date**
Federal W/H	$5854	$378.00
State W/H	$14.01	$95.40
Local W/H	$ 5.00	$34.07
FICA W/H	$31.02	$211.24
United Way	$ 2.00	$16.00
Net Pay	$389.68	

Figure 23.3. Sample pay stub.

15. A major reason for working is to make money. However, there are some people who work very hard for no remuneration. They are called "volunteers." The roles they play are vast and are much appreciated by people in nursing homes, schools, museums, and so on. Volunteers may begin when they are very young and may still be working into their senior years. Does the school have volunteers? Invite them or other volunteers to tell about their jobs and why they do them. Are there rewards other than money for their dedication? Can students in the school also become volunteers?

16. "What's My Job?" gets students to think about different occupations. Have the teacher give each child a card with an occupation on it. The other students try to guess the occupation by asking "yes" or "no" questions (e.g., Do you wear a uniform? Do you work out of doors? Do you need special training to do this job?). The number of questions can be limited so that some students will be able to "Beat the Class." Note: After a few games, students should be encouraged to suggest additional job titles.

17. Teachers may wish to use some of the activities from Chapter 19, *Night Shift Daddy*, and Chapter 14, *Mommy's Office*, to supplement or expand the activities in this chapter.

18. Word Search

These are the words in the word search (Figure 23.4, page 149).

Nurse	Roofer	Salesperson	Truck driver
Carpenter	Diver	Beautician	Librarian
Cook	Singer	Factory worker	Farmer
Soldier	Programmer		

References

Occupational Outlook Handbook (A reprint from the U.S. Department of Labor). Indianapolis: JIST Works, 1998.

The Young People's Occupational Outlook Handbook. Indianapolis: JIST Works, 2001.

```
W  I  Z  J  A  Y  Q  D  Q  Z  R  N  K  Q  L  V  Q  R  J  B
K  B  Z  R  X  C  X  R  R  J  I  C  J  N  S  M  E  B  S  H
W  G  U  A  M  I  E  E  S  A  L  E  S  P  E  R  S  O  N  F
J  N  Y  Y  W  Y  F  V  G  I  S  H  M  A  Z  N  E  Q  V  L
J  A  P  M  G  M  N  I  Q  R  E  M  R  A  F  C  U  Q  J  K
D  I  V  E  R  J  A  R  G  L  I  X  I  E  R  L  U  J  I  P
D  C  R  B  E  D  I  D  Z  N  Z  V  N  S  I  N  G  E  R  R
T  I  E  P  P  Z  R  K  S  H  Y  L  F  P  T  D  X  B  Q  G
S  T  I  D  A  K  A  C  M  Q  C  E  K  U  E  S  R  U  N  I
E  U  D  A  A  J  R  U  E  J  J  A  T  P  X  L  S  D  T  R
S  A  L  S  X  Z  B  R  X  H  J  W  X  I  K  Q  D  O  S  Q
H  E  O  X  S  T  I  T  Y  R  Q  K  V  B  U  S  L  O  Q  S
A  B  S  P  Q  M  L  R  R  B  S  I  Z  J  L  Z  N  V  T  K
Q  Q  L  I  S  X  R  E  M  M  A  R  G  O  R  P  L  Q  A  T
E  G  R  E  K  R  O  W  Y  R  O  T  C  A  F  D  E  U  O  F
T  I  I  J  D  D  K  V  E  C  C  X  M  Q  X  V  R  J  H  O
R  E  T  N  E  P  R  A  C  R  X  X  B  O  T  C  I  M  G  Q
W  H  N  F  O  U  R  K  C  A  M  D  K  G  U  P  I  Y  S  J
T  G  V  C  E  Q  X  K  K  O  O  C  S  X  F  J  F  I  Z  D
F  K  G  T  W  W  X  K  D  P  O  W  R  M  R  E  F  O  O  R
```

1. They give medical care __ __ __ __ __ __

2. They make items from wood __ __ __ __ __ __ __ __ __

3. They manage books for libraries __ __ __ __ __ __ __ __ __

4. They grow crops or raise livestock __ __ __ __ __ __ __

5. They wait on customers in a store __ __ __ __ __ __ __ __ __ __ __

6. They write instructions for the computer __ __ __ __ __ __ __ __ __

7. They cut and style hair __ __ __ __ __ __ __ __ __ __

8. They work underwater __ __ __ __ __ __

9. They assemble manufactured goods __ __ __ __ __ __ __ __ __ __ __ __ __ __

10. They prepare food in a restaurant __ __ __ __ __

11. They serve in the armed forces __ __ __ __ __ __ __ __

12. They perform vocal music __ __ __ __ __ __

13. They operate large motor vehicles which are loaded with goods __ __ __ __ __ __ __ __ __ __ __

14. They put shingles on a roof __ __ __ __ __ __ __ __

Figure 23.4 *Worksong* word search.

Appendix: Answer Keys

Chapter 1—*Albert's Field Trip*

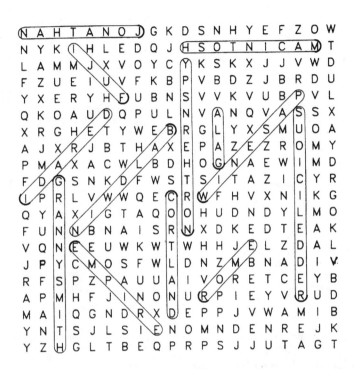

Figure A.1. Answers for Chapter 1 word search.

Chapter 2—*Potato: A Tale of the Great Depression*

Figure A.2. Map of the U.S. with state abbreviations filled in.

```
R O K Y F V X B B E B Z W Z X R P T Z D
T V F R J G A U U R K F P D W C H R W D
U J F A U H B O R L E S G U A C G A L B
E A V A W Q K B L O N M B I H Q F D M X
S T N E T N M I A S I I F T L P K E H R
F Q N H V D M T P V M J F M B F W L Y K
Q A N P Q A E P S H L M U L L U B B J K
H H L A M I V X A R A Q Z P N K B S G S
T A M Q Q L L L C Z O C Y X M L Z A L D
S S W A I F G Z R C N T Y L I I N A C
J Y D G O S E Y E C N Y H L Z W U A K W
W E M O W S W E A C W D Y P Q W E T H M
C T D X A N H C D A S H B O A R D N L B
C R P A H U U M D G G P J O B S S O K O
G M W N Z Y D E P R E S S I O N K M B Q
Z X I G K J G C Y H X N X B C N U Z K C
T C G N A T X B L T M M G I W Z C A I D
S C C T R I Z W N P H Q A H J K C C A E
E B L M O O G D E Y O L P M E N U I V S
L X M T J U Z X A L A U T O M O B I L E
```

Figure A.3. Answers for Chapter 2 word search.

Chapter 3—*The Milkman's Boy*

```
J P E Q X U L W M Y I A U K U U D L S Y
W C I U M V P A S T E U R I Z A T I O N
G M B N F A U A H B L D A D D B O M E D
F U G D P J A K M M O A K N E O K F V C
Y K R U H R H A N R K W Q N L Y T F T P
D L T L S J A W M E G X W S N N T R H H
D P H A P T K M V M R G S Y G S Q K I Q
L K O N J B O N W C D E T Z P T U E U W
X P R T K L Q G M I X M A T Q L L V R I
A Y S F E I M U I N M I B L Z E L G C L
P R E E P Z U U L B N L L X R K W N M L
H N S V A Z B E K O I K E R W A G O N O
T O L E P A T N C T I K E F M X Q D M W
Z W F R R R B P A T X O S W O N A O U B
T B V S O D Q T N L V W K D F W J B E A
S Y S P O R I J L E Y R K C E G P O E R
X I L B Q Z L U Q S Y O N S B O K W W K
C U S T O M E R S B M F A E R Y K C L V
I S S N X J T M B T D A I R Y N A K T T
W Y Z K U I C E H O U S E N J N O O J M
```

Figure A.4. Answers for Chapter 3 word search.

Chapter 4—*Mama Is a Miner*

1. d.   Tunnel
2. f.   Continuous miner
3. e.   Mantrip
4. j.   Dinner basket
5. c.   Cap light

6. g.   Working face
7. h.   Seam
8. a.   Shift
9. b.   "Safety first"
10. i.   One who shovels

Chapter 5—*Gold Fever*

Figure A.5. Answers for Chapter 5 word search.

Chapter 6—*Waiting for the Evening Star*

"You wait for that evening star now."

Chapter 7—*The Paperboy*

Figure A.6. Answers for Chapter 7 word search.

Chapter 8—*So You Want to Be President*

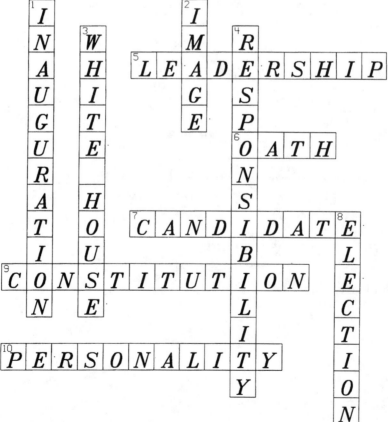

Figure A.7. Answers for Chapter 8 crossword puzzle.

Chapter 9—*Blueberries for Sal*

Individual responses will vary for the poem.

Chapter 10—*Lilly's Purple Plastic Purse*

Figure A.8. Answers for Chapter 10 word search.

Chapter 11—*A New Coat for Anna*

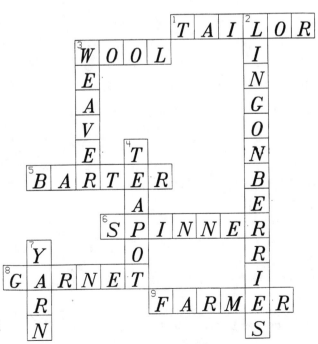

Figure A.9. Answers for Chapter 11 crossword puzzle.

Chapter 12—*Working Cotton*

"It's a long time to night."

Chapter 13—*Tomas and the Library Lady*

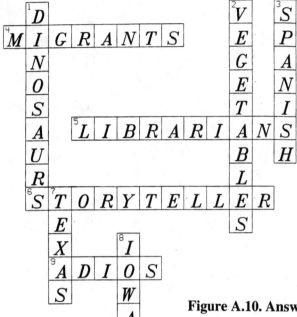

Figure A.10. Answers for Chapter 13 crossword puzzle.

Chapter 14—*Mommy's Office*

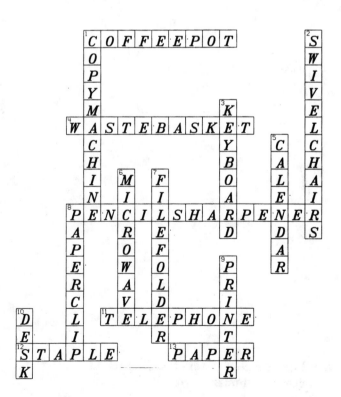

Figure A.11. Answers for Chapter 14 crossword puzzle.

Chapter 15—*Arthur's Computer Disaster*

Figure A.12. Answers for Chapter 15 crossword puzzle.

Chapter 16—*Pancakes, Pancakes*

Who Am I?

1. a. Mill
2. e. Churn
3. f. Flail
4. d. Batter
5. h. Millstone

6. i. Wheat
7. c. Flour
8. j. Straw and chaff
9. g. Miller
10. b. Pancake

Chapter 17—*Granddaddy's Street Songs*

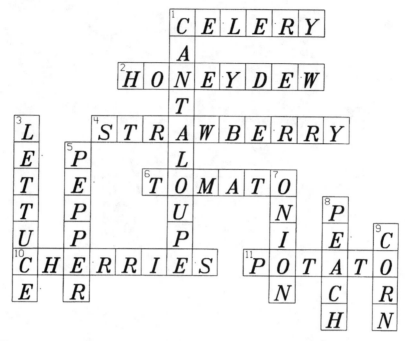

Figure A.13. Answers for Chapter 17 crossword puzzle.

Chapter 18—*Workshop*

Tool Identification

a. Hammer   1

b. Chisel   2

c. Screwdriver   6

d. Plane   5

e. Saw   3

f. Pliers   4

```
F R U B Z T R S T B T H K O C X R D K E
Y U B Z E E U V A Z Y A F Q A V O Z Y P
G O V S I I L H M L C M T D H I G T X L
A R E U U X E K K C I M L R Y Y F C T I
W D X A I D R P S F O E K E E R Q L I E
N G D Q O D A L H G G R H D R C J N V R
P T R R I E R C V L N C J N E Q U Z A S
M B I Y J O Q X C L E L B I V E Y T L U
Q F D L W J L S T Z I U G R I V E S Y L
V Z L B A R U A Z I R U S G R S U H C Y
Y A C F N W C H I S E L V C D Z N E U Z
C C X M V U O G R I K D L J W U X A D X
W W Y M I D H S N K B R L Q E Q C R M M
G M X B L W O L J S A K X V R T L S B A
G O K J X E Z V V X X R P V C Y O N T B
L W O K N H D B C W J P G I S X E T D T
K V F Q R A K R X I H M Y Z R M Q L V X
G Y Y I S X G B U D K S A W S O H P M M
M L M J V K Y H A D E M H B O D E B H E
B V P T O T J V X Y E F I N K E C V K V
```

Figure A.14. Answers for Chapter 18 word search.

Chapter 19—*Night Shift Daddy*

"How cozy are those toes?"

Chapter 20—*The Village of Round and Square Houses*

Figure A.15. Map of West Africa.

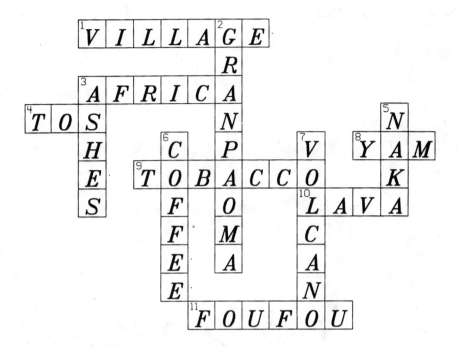

Figure A.16. Answers for Chapter 20 crossword puzzle.

Chapter 21—*Raising Yoder's Barn*

Figure A.17. Answers for Chapter 21 word search.

Chapter 22—*The Bobbin Girl*

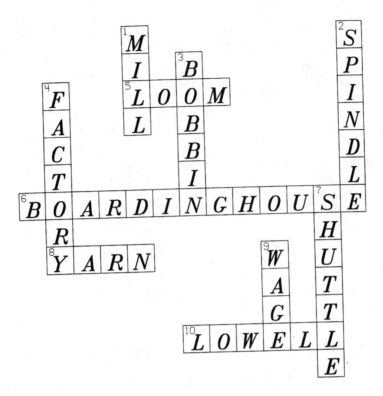

Figure A.18. Answers for Chapter 22 crossword puzzle.

Chapter 23—*Worksong*

Earning a Wage

a. $77.25

b. $38.63

c. $212.50

d. 40 hours a week at $10.00 per hour

e. 40 hours a week at $6.00 per hour

```
W I Z J A Y Q D Q Z R N K Q L V Q R J B
K B Z R X C X R R J I C J N S M E B S H
W G U A M I E E S A L E S P E R S O N F
J N Y Y W Y F V G I S H M A Z N E Q V L
J A P M G M N I Q R E M R A F C U Q J K
O I V E R J A R G L I X I E R L U J I P
D C R B E D I D Z N Z V N S I N G E R R
T I E P P Z R K S H Y L F P T D X B Q G
S T I D A K A C M Q C E K U E S R U N I
E U D A A J R U E J J A T P X L S D T R
S A L S X Z B R X H J W X I K Q D O S Q
H E O X S T I T Y R Q K V B U S L O Q S
A B S P Q M U R R B S I Z J L Z N V T K
Q Q L I S X R E M M A R G O R P L Q A T
E G R E K R O W Y R O T C A F D E U O F
T I I J D D K V E C C X M Q X V R J H O
R E T N E P R A C R X X B O T C I M G Q
W H N F O U R K C A M D K G U P I Y S J
T G V C E Q X K K O O C S X F J F I Z D
F K G T W W X K D P O W R M R E F O O R
```

Figure A.19. Answers for Chapter 23 word search.

Index

About the Authors

The Butzows live in Indiana, Pennsylvania, a small University town located in rural western Pennsylvania. One room of their home houses an extensive collection of children's and adolescent literature that provides the basis for the research involved in selecting books and developing instructional ideas included in their books about the use of literature in elementary and middle school instruction.

Carol and John both have undergraduate degrees from St. Bonaventure University in New York State. In addition, Carol completed master's degrees in history from Colgate University and in reading education from the University of Maine. Carol's doctoral degree in elementary education was earned at Indiana University of Pennsylvania. John's master's degree was earned at St. Bonaventure, and his doctorate in science education came from the University of Rochester. Carol has many years of experience teaching at the middle-junior high level, as well as at the college level. John originally worked as a teacher of science and university science educator and more recently has been a university administrator.

John and Carol have traveled extensively throughout the United States, including Alaska, to present workshops, inservice courses, and conferences. They have also spoken to audiences in Canada, Scotland, and Sweden. For information on workshops or conference presentations, please contact them through Libraries Unlimited.